Cambridge To

CW00548072

# Language Diversity and World Englishes

Dan Clayton and Rob Drummond

*Series Editors:* Dan Clayton and Marcello Giovanelli

# CAMBRIDGE
## UNIVERSITY PRESS

University Printing House, Cambridge CB2 8BS, United Kingdom

One Liberty Plaza, 20th Floor, New York, NY 10006, USA

477 Williamstown Road, Port Melbourne, VIC 3207, Australia

4843/24, 2nd Floor, Ansari Road, Daryaganj, Delhi – 110002, India

79 Anson Road, #06–04/06, Singapore 079906

Cambridge University Press is part of the University of Cambridge.

It furthers the University's mission by disseminating knowledge in the pursuit of education, learning and research at the highest international levels of excellence.

www.cambridge.org
Information on this title: www.cambridge.org/9781108402255

First published 2018

20  19  18  17  16  15  14  13  12  11  10  9  8  7  6  5  4  3  2  1

Printed in Malaysia by Vivar Printing

*A catalogue record for this publication is available from the British Library*

ISBN 978-1-108-40225-5 Paperback

# Contents

# Series introduction

*Cambridge Topics in English Language* is a series of accessible introductory study guides to major scholarly topics in the fields of English language and linguistics. These books have been designed for use by students at advanced level and beyond and provide detailed overviews of each topic together with the latest research in the field so as to provide a clear introduction that is both practical and up to date.

In all of the books in this series, we have drawn on examples of spoken and written language. We hope these will encourage you to apply the theories, concepts and methods that you will learn in the books to analyse data and to think critically about a number of issues and debates relating to language in use. Many of the books also draw on data from the Cambridge Corpus. Throughout each book, you will find short activities to help develop reading and writing skills, longer extended activities and practice questions that will enable you to explore your learning in more detail and research findings that will provide inspiration for your own language investigations. Each of the chapters includes suggested wider reading, and a full glossary and reference section at the end of each book will support you to extend your learning and provide avenues for future reading and research.

We hope that each book will give you a good overview of its topic and, that taken as a whole, the series will map out some of the most interesting and diverse areas of language study, providing you with fresh thinking and new ideas as you embark on your studies.

**Dan Clayton**

**Marcello Giovanelli**

# How to use this book

Throughout this book you will notice recurring features that are designed to help your learning. Here is a brief overview of what you'll find.

Coverage list

A short list of what you will learn in each chapter.

KEY TERM

Definitions of important terms to help your understanding of the topic.

ACTIVITY

A clearly defined task to help you apply what you've learnt.

RESEARCH QUESTION

A longer task to help you go deeper into the topic.

PRACTICE QUESTION

To give you some practice of questions you might encounter in the exam.

## Ideas and answers

Further information, suggestions and answers to activities and practice questions in the book.

## Wider reading

Key texts to help extend your learning.

# Topic introduction

One of the most interesting things about language is how it serves so many different purposes: we use it to communicate ideas, intentions, events and feelings to one another, to interact socially but also to signal aspects of our own identities. Every time we open our mouths we tell people something about ourselves, whether we know it or not.

English is a language used by many hundreds of millions of people around the world and, although we may all use it for very similar functions, the language itself can vary enormously. This book looks at that variation and subsequent linguistic diversity. It looks at the ways in which language varies from person to person, group to group and place to place, but also at the underlying functions of language, exploring why we use certain forms as well as the various features we choose. It also explores how perceptions about different kinds of language have developed over time, where these attitudes come from and how they can affect the ways we make use of certain forms of language.

In Chapter 1 the focus is on accents and dialects, examining some of the words, sounds and structures associated with different regions of the UK. It introduces some of the ways that linguists categorise sounds and you will consider the ways in which a 'standard' form of English came about and why it is such a useful tool, but such a contentious idea.

Chapter 2 looks at how language varies between individuals and social groups, examining the role of social class and age in shaping language identity. It considers the many ways in which people use specialist language in some occupations and use slang and more conversational forms in other situations.

Ethnic background is the main focus of Chapter 3. Looking at what is meant by terms such as 'race' and 'ethnicity', the chapter introduces you to key research in the field and explores the 'repertoire' of language resources available to speakers and how these are made use of to signal different aspects of identity.

Finally, Chapter 4 moves beyond the UK to consider the growth of new forms of English around the world and how they are viewed.

There is an international phonetic alphabet (IPA) chart at the end of the book to help you with the texts.

**Dan Clayton**

**Rob Drummond**

# Chapter 1
# Regional accent and dialect

In this chapter you will:

- Explore the ways in which language varies according to geographical region

- Consider what we mean by 'Standard English'

- Investigate the ways in which accent and dialect are presented in writing and performance

# 1

# 1.1 Accent and dialect

Everybody has an accent and dialect. Although you will often hear people say 'I don't really have an accent', it is actually impossible to speak without one. Accent simply refers to the way in which we pronounce the sounds that make up our speech, often in relation to geographical region. Dialect is a slightly larger term which includes the way we use vocabulary and grammar as well as pronunciation. In this chapter you will look at the ways in which accents and dialects vary, how they relate to what we know as 'Standard English', and what we feel about our accents. You will also see some examples of accent and dialect being represented in different types of writing.

> ## KEY TERMS
>
> **Accent:** variation in pronunciation, often associated with a particular geographical region
>
> **Dialect:** variation in words and structures associated with a particular geographical region (also includes accent)

One of the most important influences on both our accent and our dialect is where we grew up, with each area of a country having slightly different ways of saying some things than its neighbours, creating what we know as regional variation. The UK is particularly rich and diverse in this respect, so much so that people from one part of the country can find it difficult to understand people from another part of the country, despite the fact they are both speaking English! The reason for this rich diversity can be seen in the history of the UK, with various groups of people conquering and settling different parts of the islands at different times, each bringing their own language or dialect with them. English eventually emerged as the dominant language, but with a great deal of variation, depending on the linguistic influences of each region. (See *Language Change* in this series for more on how English has changed over time.)

Even when the various areas of the country were at relative peace, the lack of movement of people between areas due to limited transport or physical barriers meant that each region maintained its own way of speaking. Nowadays of course, people are free to move around the country with ease, and technology enables us to communicate and come into contact with people from all areas of the country and around the world. Yet the UK is still a country of great linguistic diversity; many people still speak differently depending on where they come from and, although there are some signs of accents and dialects levelling out in some respects, there is no indication at all that they will disappear.

Of course it's not just the UK that shows such variation – the USA also boasts a wide range of different accents and dialects. People sometimes think that there is more accent and dialect diversity in the UK than in the USA, but this isn't really the case. This misconception is probably due to the fact that variation in the UK happens over such a relatively small area compared to the vast size of the USA. It is true that there is less regional variation in countries like Australia and New Zealand, but that is perhaps to be expected, given the comparatively short and recent history of English in those countries. Variation takes time to develop, although it is likely that it won't develop so much in those countries anyway, given twenty-first-century levels of mobility and communication.

## 1.1.1 How do accents vary?

Certain sounds play a much greater role than others in creating variation between accents. Most variation comes from differences in vowel sounds rather than consonants, although even this is not consistent. For example, most people in the UK pronounce the vowel sound in the word 'dress' the same way no matter where they are from, whereas there is a great deal of variation in the vowel sound in the word 'goat'. Similarly, despite consonants such as 's', 'f', 'b' and 'd' being fairly consistent across all accents, other consonants such as 'k', 't' and 'th' can vary considerably.

When we discuss accents, we need a way of describing the sounds that is separate from the spelling. There are two reasons for this: firstly, unlike some languages, English spelling often does not accurately reflect English pronunciation whatever your accent (consider the word 'rough' for example) and secondly, accent variation is not normally reflected in written English, which usually follows standard conventions. Neither of these facts should come as a surprise, given that we have approximately 44 separate phonemes (sounds) in English, yet only 26 letters in the alphabet.

### KEY TERM

**Phoneme:** the smallest individual unit of sound in a language which conveys a meaning, for example in 'fell' and 'well', the /f/ and /w/ sounds are phonemes

One accurate way of describing sounds is to use the symbols of the English phonemic alphabet. In this alphabet, each phoneme of English has its own symbol. This allows us to distinguish between, for example, a northern England pronunciation of 'bus' – /bʊs/ – and a southern England pronunciation – /bʌs/. When we look up a word in a dictionary, the pronunciation is given using phonemic symbols.

1

Although phonemic symbols provide a more accurate representation of sounds than letters do, they are still not precise. This is because there is variation even within single phonemes which they can't capture. For example, listen to the way you pronounce the /l/ sound in the words 'light' and 'cool', and notice the position of your tongue and lips for each. In most accents these will be quite different sounds, yet we only have one symbol for both of them. If we wanted to show this difference we would need to use the much more detailed resource of the International Phonetic Alphabet (IPA), whose various symbols are able to describe all the sounds of any language. However, the phonemic symbols are usually enough to describe what we need when discussing differences between accents.

Another useful way of talking about the sounds of English and how they vary between accents is to use lexical sets. This is a system devised by the phonetician John Wells, who wanted a straightforward way to refer to similarities and differences between particular vowel sounds in different accents. Words are grouped together into lexical sets according to how they behave within any particular accent, and each set is represented by a keyword. For example, the keyword KIT represents a lexical set which includes words such as 'ship', 'mist' and 'visit', all words which use the /ɪ/ sound. We can therefore refer to /ɪ/ as the 'KIT' vowel.

## KEY TERM

**Lexical set:** a group of words which have the same vowel sound in a given variety of English. For example, if a particular variety uses /æ/ in the word 'bath', then it will also use /æ/ in other words within the lexical set (e.g. 'path', 'graph', etc). Each set is represented by a keyword which is usually written in SMALL CAPS

The system becomes particularly useful when describing specific accent differences, such as the variation in the word 'bus' within England. The vowel in 'bus' belongs to the lexical set STRUT, meaning that it will sound the same as the vowels in 'fun', 'must', 'come', and any other STRUT words, whatever the accent. In southern English accents, STRUT has the /ʌ/ vowel. However, in most northern English accents these words are pronounced using something close to /ʊ/, along with other words such as 'good', 'would' and 'put'. Because the lexical set system is based on southern English vowels, /ʊ/ is associated with the FOOT lexical set. See Table 1.1 to see how this works.

Table 1.1: FOOT and STRUT in southern and northern English accents

|  | STRUT<br>cut, much,<br>blood, touch | FOOT<br>put, look,<br>could, good |  |
|---|---|---|---|
| Northern English accents | /kʊt, mʊtʃ, blʊd, tʊtʃ/ | /pʊt, lʊk, kʊd, gʊd/ | No split |
| Southern English accents | /kʌt, mʌtʃ, blʌd, tʌtʃ/ | /pʊt, lʊk, kʊd, gʊd/ | Split |

Because of this separation between STRUT words ('fun', 'must', 'come') and FOOT words ('good', 'would', 'put'), we describe southern English accents as having a FOOT/STRUT split (i.e. the words in each of these sets are pronounced with two different vowels). On the other hand, northern English accents, which use the same vowel for both groups of words, are described as lacking a FOOT/STRUT split. Incidentally, the reason this is described as a 'split' is because the northern pronunciation was the original one hundreds of years ago, and the southern one represents a change that took place in which some words took on a new vowel.

Figure 1.1: The approximate border between northern and southern English uses of FOOT/STRUT (based on the map from Chambers and Trudgill, 1998).

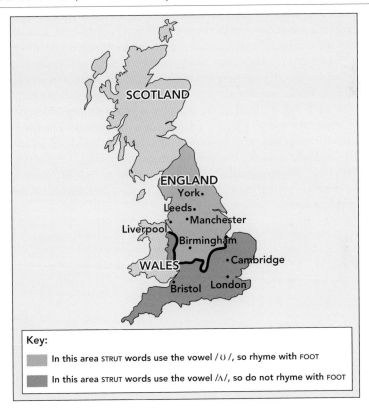

Key:

In this area STRUT words use the vowel / ʊ /, so rhyme with FOOT

In this area STRUT words use the vowel /ʌ/, so do not rhyme with FOOT

5

# Language Diversity and World Englishes

The full list of lexical sets can be seen in Table 1.2, along with some example words. The phonemic symbols next to each represents the sound of the vowel in the accents known as Received Pronunciation (RP) or General American (GA). These two accents often serve as models for teaching English, and are represented in dictionary pronunciations of words. If you would like to hear the sounds represented by the symbols, there are plenty of resources online such as the interactive phonemic charts by Macmillan.
RP: www.cambridge.org/links/escdiv6001
GA: www.cambridge.org/links/escdiv6002

## KEY TERMS

**Received Pronunciation (RP):** an accent in English which does not indicate a person's geographical location and which is recognised as having a high social status; RP is found throughout the English-speaking world

**General American (GA):** The majority accent in the USA, lacking any distinctly regional characteristics. It is an imprecise term that is used in linguistics mainly for comparison purposes

As you can see, several of the sets have the same RP phonemic symbol, meaning that in an RP accent they are pronounced with the same vowel. However, the fact that the different sets exist means that in some accents at least, they are pronounced differently. Similarly, some of the sets have different symbols in RP, yet they would have the same symbol in another accent (for example, NURSE and SQUARE in Liverpool English). It is worth bearing in mind that while all of the sets play a role in distinguishing between accents, some of the examples are only relevant to American English (John Wells used RP and General American as his reference 'standard' accents when he originally compiled the list). For example, in many US accents, LOT and CLOTH have different vowels (LOT is usually close to /ɑː/ (RP PALM) while CLOTH is close to /ɔ/ (RP THOUGHT)), whereas in most British accents they have the same vowel.

Table 1.2: A list of lexical sets and example words for Received Pronunciation (RP) and General American (GA)

| Keyword | RP | GA | Example words | Keyword | RP | GA | Example words |
|---|---|---|---|---|---|---|---|
| KIT | ɪ | ɪ | ship, sick, lift, build | GOOSE | uː | u | loop, mute, spoon, who |
| DRESS | e | ɛ | step, bell, death, said | PRICE | aɪ | aɪ | like, die, ice, ride |
| TRAP | æ | æ | cat, dash, tax, ant | CHOICE | ɔɪ | ɔɪ | noise, join, boy, void |
| LOT | ɒ | ɑ | odd, font, swan, wasp | MOUTH | aʊ | aʊ | out, house, count, browse |
| STRUT | ʌ | ʌ | cut, much, blood, touch | NEAR | ɪə | ɪr | deer, fear, here, ear |
| FOOT | ʊ | ʊ | put, look, could, good | SQUARE | eə | ɛr | care, pear, where, their |
| BATH | ɑː | æ | path, daft, dance, laugh | START | ɑː | ɑr | sharp, large, carve, heart |
| CLOTH | ɒ | ɔ | cough, broth, long, cross | NORTH | ɔː | ɔr | for, war, short, scorch |
| NURSE | ɜː | ɜr | hurt, church, girl, stern | FORCE | ɔː | or | four, wore, porch, born |
| FLEECE | iː | i | creep, meet, speak, key | CURE | ʊə* | ʊr | pure, tourist, lure, sure |
| FACE | eɪ | eɪ | cake, late, name, weight | happY | i | i | city, busy, copy, sorry |
| PALM | ɑː | ɑ | calm, father, spa, lager | lettER | ə | ər | paper, centre, order, donor |
| THOUGHT | ɔː | ɔ | taught, sauce, fought, jaw | commA | ə | ə | vodka, quota, panda, sofa |
| GOAT | əʊ | oʊ | soap, oak, know, rogue | | | | *This is now quite an old-fashioned pronunciation. Most 'RP' speakers now use /ɔː/ as in NORTH for this set. |

In addition to the differences between FOOT and STRUT described in Table 1.1, Table 1.3 shows a few of the more salient variations in British English accents.

Table 1.3: Some examples of accent differences in British English

| | |
|---|---|
| BATH and TRAP | Separate in southern England, the same in northern England. |
| NURSE and SQUARE | Pronounced with the same vowel in areas of the north-west of England. Interestingly, some areas (e.g. parts of Lancashire) use the /ɜː/ vowel for both, whereas other areas (e.g. parts of Merseyside) use /ɛː/ for both. |
| LOT and THOUGHT | Pronounced with the same vowel in most Scottish accents, so *cot* and *caught* are homophones. |
| *happy* | Many northern English accents have /ɪ/ for the vowel at the end of these words while southern English accents tend to have /i/ or /iː/. |
| FACE and GOAT | Many northern English accents have long monophthongs for these words – /feːs/, /goːt/. |

## ACTIVITY 1.1
### Your accent

Look at the words in the table of lexical sets (Table 1.2). How does your pronunciation compare to those of the RP or GA examples? Do you have any of the differences described in Table 1.3? Can you identify any other regional variations based on what you've heard on TV or in the media? For example, how do some people from Manchester (UK) typically pronounce the *lett*ER vowel?

If English is your second language, are you aware of having a British or American accent? How does your pronunciation compare to the pronunciations in Table 1.2?

In both cases it might be helpful to first listen to some recordings of example RP and GA vowels found online (e.g. www.cambridge.org/links/escdiv6003).

Whilst it's mostly vowel sounds which vary between accents, some consonant sounds do too. Sometimes there are sounds which used to be associated with particular regional areas, but have spread to other areas. For example, th-fronting, where people use /f/ or /v/ for 'th' in words such as 'three' or 'brother' used to be thought of as a London feature, but now it can be heard all over the UK. Other times there are sounds which remain very much associated with a particular region, for example the /t/ sound in Liverpool English which can sound a bit like /ts/ in words such as 'tree' or 'ten'.

Another very important feature which distinguishes English accents is the use of postvocalic /r/. Postvocalic /r/ is the name given to an /r/ sound that comes after a vowel. It is there in the spelling, for example in words such as 'car' and 'park', but is not always sounded in speech. Most accents in England don't pronounce this sound, with only relatively small areas (parts of the north-west and parts of the south-west) clinging on to what used to be a widespread feature of British English. However, it is still the usual pronunciation for most Scottish, Irish and US accents of English. Accents which do pronounce the /r/ are known as rhotic accents.

## KEY TERMS

**Monophthong:** a vowel which has a single sound throughout its duration. For example, the /iː/ vowel sound in the word 'sheep'

**Th-fronting:** the pronunciation of 'th' as /f/ or /v/. So 'think' becomes 'fink' and 'with' becomes 'wiv'

**Postvocalic /r/:** the /r/ sound that appears after a vowel and before a consonant ('farm') or at the end of a word ('far'). It is not pronounced in most English accents

**Rhotic accent:** an accent which pronounces postvocalic /r/

## ACTIVITY 1.2
### Accent survey

Devise a survey which will enable you to analyse different people's accents. If you are able to talk to the people face-to-face and record their speech you could simply ask them to read a list of words, or perhaps a few sentences. Make sure you have included a few examples of those words which you think are likely to vary according to accent. If you have time, you could also try to record the same people speaking more naturally in conversation (remember to ask permission and explain what the recording is for). Why do you think this might be important?

If you are not able to speak to people face-to-face, you could try devising some questions which will tell you about their accent. A good way to do this is by asking if certain words rhyme in their speech. For example:

• Do the words 'hut' and 'foot' rhyme in your speech?

- Do you pronounce the words 'fur' and 'fair' the same?

- Do you pronounce the words 'paw' and 'pour' the same?

When you have finished, compare the accents. Are they different? In what ways?

If you do not have access to people who have different English accents, try to analyse videos of people speaking instead. Listen out for some keywords which you think are likely to vary. Make a note of how they are pronounced. If you don't know the phonemic symbol, or if you can't describe the difference, try to replicate the pronunciation yourself and notice what changes. For example, is your mouth more open? Is there more/less movement of your tongue?

## 1.1.2 Lexical variation

All of the examples so far have been to do with accent; however, there is also a great deal of regional dialect variation in the UK. After accent, perhaps the most noticeable differences occur at the level of lexis, with people from different areas of the country having different words for even the most everyday things. Probably the most well-known area of disagreement is the one surrounding the item pictured in Figure 1.2. Depending on where someone grew up, this could be a picture of a bread roll, a barm, a morning roll, a bap, a batch, a cob, a scuffler, a stotty, or a buttery. And what about those things on your feet – are they trainers, runners, sneakers, joggers, sandshoes, plimsolls, pumps, creps, or kickers? No doubt you have a clear idea about the differences between what some of these words refer to, but the interesting thing is that these differences vary from region to region. It's not just that people from different places use different words for some things, rather that people from different places often use the same words for different things!

Figure 1.2: What do you call these?

Linguist Carmen Llamas (2007) came up with a good method of investigating lexical variation, by using Sense Relation Networks (SRNs). This approach draws on the idea that there exists a network of interconnected words and phrases in our minds. The task involves the interviewer leading the participants (this kind of research is often done in pairs) around the various semantic fields, encouraging them to discuss and explore their own dialect words and the various connotations they have. Figure 1.3 shows a completed SRN (Llamas, Mullany and Stockwell 2006). This kind of research can be very useful in uncovering patterns of lexical variation both across regions, but also across different social groups within the same region. For example, it is likely that you would get different answers from a person in their 80s than you would from a teenager, even if they grew up in the same area.

**Figure 1.3: A Sense Relation Network, completed by a research participant**

# 1.1.3 Grammatical variation

Regional variation also occurs at the level of grammar. Arthur Hughes, Peter Trudgill and Dominic Watt describe some of the differences in their book *English Accents and Dialects* (2012). This is a very useful book which they update every few years, adding new areas and additional detail each time. The examples in the book show how sometimes the grammatical differences between regional dialects can be relatively small, perhaps only consisting of a variation in the way contractions are used. For example, while southern British English accents tend to use phrases of the type: 'I haven't got it; She won't go; Doesn't he like it?', northern British English accents are more likely to use: 'I've not got it; She'll not go; Does he not like it?'

While this kind of variation is generally accepted as falling within Standard English (see below), other types of grammatical variation are more stigmatised. For example, multiple negation (e.g. 'I didn't do nothing') is certainly non-standard, as is a phrase like 'I was stood next to her', but both can be routinely heard in various regions of the UK. Here are some other common examples of non-standard grammar (adapted from Hughes, Trudgill and Watt 2012):

- **The verb *to be*.** Whereas Standard English follows the pattern *I was, you were, he/she/it was, we were, they* were, several areas of the country (including London) use the non-standard pattern *I was, you was, he/she/ it was, we was, they was*. In complete contrast, some northern regional varieties use the pattern: *I were, you were, he/she/it were, we were, they were*. An excellent resource for seeing and hearing all sorts of regional variation is the British Library's 'Sounds familiar' website: www.cambridge. org/links/escdiv6004. It even has a map of *was/were* variation with examples from around the country: www.cambridge.org/links/escdiv6005.

- **African American English (AAE) habitual *be*.** In AAE, the sentence 'She be getting angry' does not mean 'She is getting angry (now)' but rather 'She often/regularly/is always getting angry'.

- **Present tense verb forms.** The Standard English pattern is actually quite strange, insisting on an extra 's' for third-person singular form (*he/she/it*): *I play, you play, she plays*, etc. Some non-standard dialects don't have this difference. For example, in East Anglia and in some Caribbean varieties of English, we get: 'She play football'; 'He want to go'; 'It make me sad'. However, in other parts of the UK, the opposite happens, with everything using 's'. In the south-west of England and south Wales for example, we might hear: 'I likes it'; 'You gives it to her'; 'We goes to the pub'.

- **Determiners.** While Standard English has 'Look at those people', various non-standard dialects use 'Look at them people'. In some Scottish dialects, both *those* and *these* can be replaced with *thae* (or *they*): 'Give me thae books'.

# 1.2 Standard English

Most people have a concept of some kind of a 'standard' English, the variety that is used in print, in education, and in government and legal contexts. Often it is viewed as the variety of English which is most 'correct', and therefore the variety which is 'better' than any other varieties. Linguists don't see it this way. Yes, there is a recognised standard variety of English, but this variety is simply another dialect, no better or worse than any other dialect of English. Its 'standardness' comes from status rather than quality, and this status was itself acquired indirectly through accidents of history. The truth is, as in all languages, the prestige variety is the variety associated with whoever happens to have the power in any given society. The power in the UK, at least since the eleventh century, has centred in and around London; therefore, it was the variety of English that emerged in that region of the country that came to be seen as the most prestigious. This is then the variety that became standardised and reinforced through the process of printing and publishing, thereby making all other varieties by definition 'non-standard'.

But even a standard variety of a language is not fixed, and people continually argue over what is and isn't acceptable. Some people imagine that there exists somewhere an organisation or committee that decides what is or isn't 'correct' English (France actually has the *Académie Française* for this purpose, although its role is largely symbolic). But in reality, the 'rules' of Standard English are created by the grammarians who publish the books, and while these days there is much more interest in how language is *actually* used (a descriptive approach), in the past there was much more emphasis on how language *should* be used (a prescriptive approach). The only problem was, different authors often had very different ideas as to what was or wasn't acceptable, resulting in a whole lot of contradictory 'rules', some of which are still causing confusion today.

## KEY TERMS

**Descriptivism:** an approach to language study that focuses on how language is actually used

**Prescriptivism:** an approach to language study that focuses on rules and notions of correctness

It is actually very easy to illustrate why we shouldn't think of Standard English as being any better than all the other non-standard dialects. The fact is, from a purely linguistic perspective, various non-standard dialects are actually more sophisticated than the standard. For example, unlike many other languages, Standard English has no way of differentiating between singular and plural second-person personal pronouns: 'Where have *you* been?' could be referring to one person or several. However, various non-standard dialects do have the distinction: using 'Where have *youse* been?' refers to more than one person. Non-standard, but definitely not sub-standard.

In a lecture organised by Cambridge University Press (2012), linguist David Crystal had this to say about Standard English:

> Standard English is the minority dialect, always has been. Perhaps 1% of the English speakers of the world use Standard English. I should say of course English writers of the world because Standard English is essentially the dialect of the written language, defined as you know by its grammar, by its spelling, and its punctuation, and to a minor extent by vocabulary as well. If people say 'What is Standard English?' we give examples, and there are dozens of them like: in Standard English we don't use double negatives, for example. Nobody in Standard English says 'I haven't got nothing'....
> But that written language, that written definition of standard is still only a minority of the overall English language use in the world. Nobody's got any real statistics of course, but how many people speak Standard English in that way? I'm doing my best at the moment, and indeed you will hear Standard English spoken on the most public of occasions and that's why everybody gets the impression that it's universal. But in actual fact perhaps only 5% at most of the spoken English around the world is going to be Standard English.

Most people speak a mixture of Standard English and some kind of local dialect, but the precise make-up and balance of that mixture is influenced by all sorts of social factors. Location (region), social class, level of education, occupation, age and gender all play a role in determining how close to the standard our language might be. Perhaps the most important influencing factor is the context in which we are speaking – who we are speaking to and for what purpose.

So far, we have looked at the idea of Standard English in relation to dialect, but what about accent? The closest we have to a Standard English accent is Received Pronunciation (RP). Although historically it has its origins in the speech of the areas around London, RP is an accent of prestige and higher social position rather than of any particular region. It is the model used in the teaching of English as a second language, and is the accent often associated with BBC newsreaders and the Queen ('BBC English' and 'The Queen's English' are sometimes used informally as alternative terms for RP). However, RP has changed over the years; just listen to clips of BBC newsreaders from the 1950s to get an idea of how much. In fact, even the Queen's accent has altered over time.

Linguist Jonathan Harrington has tracked changes in various aspects of the Queen's accent by analysing her recorded Christmas speeches over a 50-year period, concluding that certain aspects of her speech have moved towards a more general southern British English variety. This BBC story – 'Has the Queen become frightfully common?' discusses some of Harrington's findings, and provides some videos of the Queen for comparison: www.cambridge.org/links/escdiv6006.

Although RP is changing, its value as a pronunciation model for people learning English is not really in any doubt, as long as dictionaries and teaching materials reflect those changes as they occur. After all, it wouldn't really be fair to teach people in 2017 to speak in the RP accent of the Queen in the 1950s! However, similar to the idea of a Standard English dialect discussed earlier, RP should not be thought of as being any 'better' than any other accent – it is simply the standardised model of pronunciation that has emerged as a result of historical chance. If York (a city in the north-east of England) happened to be the capital of the country rather than London (in south-east England), there is every likelihood that the prestige accent of England would be very different. There would likely be no FOOT/STRUT split for a start!

When we talk of prestige in relation to the idea of a standard dialect or model of pronunciation, we are referring to what's known as overt prestige. Overt prestige comes from the acceptance of this or that (standard) variety as being valued and accepted in a particular society. On the other hand, a non-standard variety might have covert prestige, meaning that despite possibly being stigmatised in wider society, it is valued for other reasons within smaller social groups of people. Often this positive evaluation is unconscious, with people claiming not to use such a variety when asked. Gerard Van Herk, a sociolinguist, defines the two types of prestige in this way:

**Overt prestige:** positive or negative assessments of variants that are in line with the dominant norms associated with sounding 'proper' and that people are aware of, often coinciding with the norms of the media, educational institutions, or higher socio-economic classes.

**Covert prestige:** a norm or target the speakers unconsciously orient to, with a sort of hidden positive evaluation that speakers give to other (presumably non-standard) forms. The linguistic equivalent of *street credibility*. (Van Herk 2012)

## KEY TERMS

**Overt prestige:** the obvious prestige associated with the use of the standard variety of a language within a particular society. Connected to notions of speaking 'properly'

**Covert prestige:** the less obvious or hidden prestige associated with the use of certain non-standard varieties of a language within particular social groups. Van Herk (2012: 55) calls it 'the linguistic equivalent of *street credibility*'

*[handwritten margin note: Received Pronunciation (Standard English accent)]*

# 1.3 Accent loss and maintenance

Stories frequently appear in the media about UK accents and dialects disappearing, concluding that soon we are all going to sound the same. This process of dialect levelling certainly does occur, but the outcome is perhaps not so inevitable as some of the stories suggest. The fact is that while some linguistic features may gradually disappear from a particular location and be replaced by more widespread variants, other features remain firmly in place. More than this, at the same time as linguists are tracking how various items seem to be being used less and less, it is undoubtedly the case that new ways of speaking are emerging (usually among young people), which may in time prove to be just as region-specific.

## KEY TERM

**Dialect levelling:** the process by which language forms of different parts of the country converge and become more similar over time, with the loss of regional features and reduced diversity of language

One of the reasons that regional variation persists is the role such variation plays in our own sense of identity. Our language, particularly the way we speak, is a big part of who we are and how we are perceived by others. It therefore makes sense that if somebody has a strong sense of regional identity, then this will be displayed in their speech. Some linguists see our speech as reflecting our identities: for example, a person speaks this way because she is a teenager from Derby. However, more recent thinking suggests that language is just another way in which we 'perform' our identities: a person creates a 'teenage' and 'Derby' identity through the way they speak, in the same way as they might perform their affiliation to a particular social group through the way they dress and the music they listen to, in addition to the language they use.

Thinking of language and identity in this way helps us to understand why it is that we often change the way we speak depending on who we are interacting with. Most of us are fully aware of the fact that we usually speak differently to our friends than we would to a teacher for example, but what about if we find ourselves speaking to people with whom we don't share an accent? For many people the first time this happens is when we go away to university or get a job in another part of the country. In these situations it is normal to suddenly feel very aware of our regional accent, and other people may comment on the way we speak. What often happens is that we then soften our accent slightly, perhaps in order to be understood more clearly, perhaps in order to fit in. But then when we next go home, we immediately slip back into our old way of speaking. In each situation, we are using language as a way of performing and maintaining our particular individual and group identities, and geographical region can often play a big part in this.

# 1.4 Accent and dialect in print and performance

Eye dialect is the term given to writing which uses non-standard spelling in order to portray non-standard (often regional) accents and dialects. You can find it in all sorts of writing, from novels, to poems, to cartoons, and when done well, the effect can be very striking. In this section we are going to look at some examples from a variety of sources.

## KEY TERM

**Eye dialect:** the deliberate use of misspellings to identify a speaker who is using a regional or non-standard form of English. So called because we see rather than hear the difference

## 1.4.1 Written texts

### Poetry

Ian McMillan is a poet from Barnsley in Yorkshire. He speaks with a strong local accent, and his writing, especially when it is about Yorkshire life, reflects this.

Figure 1.4

# Language Diversity and World Englishes

## Text 1A

From under't canal like a watter-filled cellar

coming up like a pitman from a double'un, twice.

I said "Hey, you're looking poorly"

He said "Them nights are drawing in"

Down't stairs like a gob-machine, sucking toffees,

up a ladder like a ferret up a ladder in a fog,

I said "Hey, you're looking poorly"

He said "Half-a-dozen eggs"

Over't top in't double-decker groaning like a whippet

like a lamplighter's daughter in a barrel full of milk,

I said "Hey, you're looking poorly"

He said "Night's a dozen eggs"

Down't canal like a barrow full of Gillis's parsnips,

coming up like a cage of men in lit-up shiny hats,

I said "Hey, you're looking poorly"

He said "Half a dozen nights"

Under't canal on a pushbike glowing like an eggshell

up a ladder wi' a pigeon and a broken neck,

I said "Hey, you're looking poorly"

He said "I feel like half-a-dozen eggs"

Over't night on a shiny bike wi' a lit-up hat,

perfect for't poorly wi' heads like eggs,

I said "Hey, you died last week"

He said "Aye, did you miss me?"

Ian McMillan, 'The Meaning of Life (A Yorkshire Dialect Rhapsody)'
from *Now It Can Be Told* (Carcanet, 1983)

## ACTIVITY 1.3

### Writing in your own accent

How does the accent represented in Text 1A deviate from RP, or from your own accent? If your accent is different, how would you use spellings to represent these and other words to match the way you speak? If you are from Barnsley yourself, or know somebody who is, how accurate do you think this representation of the accent is?

Look online for some more examples of dialect poetry – or write a poem of your own!

## Comic strips

*The Broons* and *Oor Wullie* are comic strips which appear in the Scottish newspaper *The Sunday Post*. Both are written in local Scottish dialect, based on that of a fictitious Scottish industrial town.

Look at Text 1B (from *The Broons*) and Text 1C (from *Oor Wullie*). Notice how the writing is a mixture of accent spellings (e.g. 'oor') and dialect spellings (e.g. 'neeps', meaning parsnips/swedes).

Text 1B

### Transliteration (from left to right)

The haggis is set on the table for our Burns' supper.

Oh, not that again – boring haggis, parsnips/swedes* and potatoes. And you all reciting daft poems.

And making that awful racket with bagpipes and fiddles.

It's not fair – you did this to us last year.

I think we're losing the young ones.

It's time we took a thought to ourselves [it's time we had a think/thought about it]

Yes, we could make some small changes.

I'm up for it. What do you have in mind?

*Interestingly, there is another dialect difference here, as the two vegetables are named in the opposite way to each other in many English and Scottish dialects!

*The Broons, The Sunday Post*, 22 January 2017

## Text 1C

**Transliteration**

In Rio, far from Scotland's cold, our warrior brought home the gold.

*Oor Wullie, The Sunday Post*, 22 January 2017

## Stories and novels

American novelist Thomas Wolfe wrote the (very) short story 'Only the Dead Know Brooklyn' in 1935 (Text 1D). It's not so much a story as a sketch, a slice of life in the form of a narrated conversation about Brooklyn, New York, between two men on a train. What makes it special however, is that it's written entirely in 'Brooklynese' from that period. (The underlined words are explained in the glossary.)

**Text 1D**

Dere's no guy livin' dat knows Brooklyn <u>t'roo an' t'roo</u>, because it'd take a guy a lifetime just to find his way aroun' duh goddam town.

So like I say, I'm waitin' for my train t' come when I sees dis big guy standin' <u>deh</u>—dis is duh <u>foist</u> I eveh see of him. Well, he's lookin' wild, y'know, an' I can see dat he's had plenty, but still he's holdin' it; he talks good an' is walkin' straight enough. So den, dis big guy steps up to a little guy dat's standin' deh, an' says, "How d'yuh get t' Eighteent' Avenoo an' Sixty-sevent' Street?" he says.

"Jesus! Yuh got me, chief," duh little guy says to him. "I ain't been <u>heah</u> long myself. Where is duh place?" he says. "Out in duh Flatbush section somewhere?"

"Nah," duh big guy says. "It's out in Bensenhoist. But I was neveh deh befoeh. How d'yuh get deh?"

"Jesus," duh little guy says, scratchin' his head, y'know—yuh could see duh little guy didn't know his way about—"yuh got me, chief. I neveh <u>hoid</u> of it. Do any of youse guys know where it is?" he says to me.

"Sure," I says. "It's out in Bensenhoist. Yuh take duh Fourt' Avenoo express, get off at Fifty-nint' Street, change to a Sea Beach local deh, get off at Eighteent' Avenoo an' Sixty-toid, an' den walk down <u>foeh</u> blocks. Dat's all yuh got to do," I says.

Thomas Wolfe, 'Only the Dead Know Brooklyn',
*The New Yorker,* 15 June 1935

## Glossary

| | |
|---|---|
| *t'roo an' t'roo* | through and through |
| *deh* | there |
| *foist* | first |
| *heah* | here |
| *hoid* | heard |
| *foeh* | four |

## 1.4.2 Spoken text

### Songs and lyrics

The vast majority of popular music is performed using some kind of generic American English accent. It's not entirely clear why this should be the case, but it's probably a combination of two factors, one social, one phonetic. Socially, there is a sense that singers are using the style that suits the music – pop and rock music, with its roots in American Blues and Rock 'n' Roll, has always been sung in that way. Singers are therefore continuing a tradition, or abiding by the (unwritten) rules of the genre. Phonetically, there is an argument that the process of singing tends to reduce or remove the various qualities of speech that make up an accent (vowel quality, rhythm, intonation), leaving a neutral accent that just happens to sound American. David Crystal discusses these influences on his blog: www.cambridge.org/links/escdiv6007. There is also an interesting short video on the subject from *Slate* magazine, 'Why Do British Singers Sound American, Like Adele on "Skyfall"?': www.cambridge.org/links/escdiv6008.

Of course there have always been exceptions, especially when part of the singer's or group's identity is deliberately tied to a specific region. Some recent (and not so recent) examples include Lily Allen (London), Madness (London), Arctic Monkeys (Sheffield), Kasabian (Leicester) and Sleaford Mods (Nottingham/Lincolnshire). However, there appears to be something of a surge in regional accent performance, at least in one particular genre: grime. Grime is a style of music that grew out of early 2000s East London. Whilst there are similarities to hip hop (both styles involve rapping), grime has its roots in different styles of music such as garage, bashment and dancehall. Although grime artists all tend to perform in something close to Multicultural London English (see Chapter 3), it is undoubtedly the case that certain regional accent and dialect features are retained in the performance of certain non-London artists. Two high-profile examples are Bugzy Malone from Manchester and Lady Leshurr from Birmingham. And for Lady Leshurr at least, it is a conscious decision to use her own accent. Speaking in an interview with *Dazed and Confused* magazine in 2016, she said: 'People used to diss my accent and I got insecure and stopped using it. But I just woke up one day and thought, "What are you doing Leesh? You're from Birmingham, you shouldn't have to hide your accent because of other people"': www.cambridge.org/links/escdiv6009.

### RESEARCH QUESTION

#### Regional accent in music

Try to find some more examples of singers/rappers/groups who use their own regional accents in their performances. What is it precisely that makes it noticeable? Is it a particular vowel sound? Is it consistent throughout their tracks? Why do you think they are doing this? Is it making a statement about regional identity?

Alternatively, look at some artists from other countries who perform in English. Do they tend to use an American accent or another type of accent? Why do you think this is?

In this chapter you have seen what it is that actually varies when we talk about regional accent and dialect variation, and how we can best describe these differences. You also now have some ideas and techniques for investigating the differences yourself. You have been introduced to the notion of Standard English, suggesting that its position of prestige, along with RP, is nothing to do with any linguistic superiority. You touched upon the role which regional accent and dialect play in making us who we are, before finally looking at some of the ways in which accent and dialect are portrayed in writing and music. In the next chapter you will look further into how language is used and how it varies in relation to the social groups we belong to and identity with.

# Wider reading

You can find out more about the topics in this chapter by reading or listening to the following:

Fry, S. (2008–17), *Fry's English Delight*, series on BBC Radio 4: www.bbc.co.uk/programmes/b00lv1k1/episodes/player

Hughes, A., Trudgill, P. and Watt, D. (2012) *English Accents and Dialects* (Fifth edition). London: Routledge.

Kamm, O. (2015) *Accidence Will Happen: The Non-Pedantic Guide to English Usage.* London: Orion Publishing.

Trudgill, P. (1999) *The Dialects of England* (Second edition). Oxford: Blackwell.

# Chapter 2
# Language
# and social groups

In this chapter you will:

- Look at the ways in which different groups of people use language

- Evaluate research into the language of social groups

- Explore the varying functions and uses of language in a range of contexts

# 2.1 Idiolect and sociolect

In the last chapter you looked at the ways in which language varies from place to place and how this is manifested in different linguistic features such as accents and dialects, and features of Standard or non-Standard English. In this chapter, you will consider how language varies from person to person, not just on an individual level but how each one of us belongs to certain identifiable groups and how that affects and shapes our language.

It has been well established by linguists that each individual has their own individual language style, be it their tone of voice, handwriting, use of certain phrases and vocabulary items, or their use of particular grammatical or interactive constructions. An individual's own language style is known as an idiolect. In some cases, this idiolect is instantly recognisable: think of familiar presenters on the TV or radio and you might be able to hear a person's voice and even their catchphrases or vocal cadences, without trying too hard. Think of your own immediate family: do your parents, grandparents or siblings have ways of talking that are instantly recognisable as their own?

Some linguists have argued that each of us has a linguistic fingerprint – a style of language that is unique to each of us and that can be used to identify us – and have gone as far as to suggest that in the future we will all be identifiable by the language we use. Writing about the field of forensic linguistics, Malcolm Coulthard argues that this is still some way off. However, he notes:

> Every speaker has a very large active vocabulary built up over many years, which will differ from the vocabularies others have similarly built up not only in terms of actual items but also in preferences for selecting certain items rather than others. Thus, whereas in principle any speaker/writer can use any word at any time, speakers in fact tend to make typical and individuating co-selections of preferred words. (Coulthard 2004)

But individuals are not just born speaking differently; we develop language in interaction with people around us and from the communities we are part of, and this leads us to the concept of sociolect. If idiolect is an individual language style, then sociolect is a language style associated with a social group.

## KEY TERMS

**Idiolect:** variation in language use associated with an individual's personalised 'speech style'

**Sociolect:** the language used by a particular social group, e.g. teenage school children, adults in a book club

The term 'social group' can be slippery to define, but we are all members of different groups, whether we want to be or not. People might share characteristics such as social background, age, occupation, interests and activities, and these help to classify them into groups. Additionally, many of these groups overlap, so it might be argued that people belong to a number of different social groups at the same time and that their language is often shaped by – and sometimes constructed through – the groups that they belong to.

For example, people who play online games such as *World of Warcraft*, *The Elder Scrolls* or *RuneScape*, belong to a social group, even if they do not personally know the other people they are playing with (because it's carried out through an internet connection, rather than face to face), and will inevitably share some of the language characteristics of that group because they are engaged together in the same activity. This will probably consist of vocabulary items related to the games they play and the locations and characters within them, but also a set of terms that might be familiar to players of other games of this genre, such as 'RPG' (role-playing game), 'tank' (a character who is heavily armoured and can cause a lot of damage to opponents), 'boss' (a top-level enemy) or 'mobs' (monsters that appear in larger numbers in a game). As well as this field-specific lexis, gamers will use language to describe their reactions in a game and to describe their fellow gamers (and opponents).

The nature of online chat varies, depending on whether it uses Voice Over Internet Protocol (VOIP), which is spoken language relayed from one player to others, or chat messages, which rely on keyboards and online 'writing'. The platform or mode being used can have an influence here, so gamers who are playing without speaking to collaborators or competitors may well be typing short abbreviated messages such as GG (good game), AFK (away from keyboard) or more widely recognised terms such as LOL (laughing out loud) and ROFL (rolling on floor laughing). Those speaking over an internet connection might not use as many of these abbreviations (because they do not need to shorten what they are saying for ease of communication) but might instead have a particular style of interaction and turn taking with other players that is very much part of the activity they are involved in.

## KEY TERMS

**Field-specific lexis:** vocabulary that is only related to a particular field of work or activity

**Mode:** the physical channel of communication: either speech or writing

On the other hand, a social group that an individual is part of might have little connection with their interests and be more closely related to their personal background. Social class is something that can define our life chances and even life expectancy, but it is also a significant influence on language. We will look in more detail at a range of areas – occupational groups and social class among them – later in this chapter, but first we will need to think about what we mean by social groups and the reasons for different forms of language being used within them.

## 2.1.1 Language and social identity

While one of the main functions of language is to communicate ideas and feelings from one person to others (a transactional function), language also fulfils an important role in signalling identity (an interpersonal function). On one level, the language choices made by an individual can signal something about them as individuals and the persona they would like to project, whether it is respectful, polite, relaxed, rebellious, cautious, caring or excited, but on another level the language choices of an individual can also signal a complex range of connections between an individual, other individuals and the society they are part of (or in some cases, see themselves as separate from).

Think about the various different words that exist to describe what would be termed (in Standard English) as the police. A variety of terms is used nowadays to describe police officers and many more have been used in the past. Some of these signal respect for authority: 'Members of Her Majesty's Constabulary' might be such a term, where the deliberate reference to the Queen places the police officer's role within a traditional British hierarchy. However, the 'Old Bill' (a term dating back to the 1950s, according to Jonathon Green's *Dictionary of Slang* (2010)) is less respectful and perhaps brings to mind (to people of a certain age and social background) the slang of criminals from London's East End. If you were to describe the police as the 'Feds' or 'Po-po', it might suggest an American or African-American influence on your language, and perhaps signal a disdain for their work, while describing the police as 'the filth' would be seen as extremely disrespectful. However, by using a particular term, an individual is signalling a great deal about their attitudes to society and their affiliation (or otherwise) to what might be perceived as its mainstream values. While it might not be socially acceptable in mainstream society to refer to the police as 'the filth' in formal conversation, the use of the term in some situations might confer a degree of covert prestige upon the speaker among some of their friends. By using this term, a social identity might be conferred on the speaker that is seen to be at odds with mainstream social values. Whether the person saying it is a middle class, privately-educated farmer's daughter or the working class son of a career criminal, the use of the language signifies something about the identity that speaker would like to have, would like to project and the groups he or she would like to identify with.

Julie Coleman, in *The Life of Slang* (2012), suggests a scenario in which a white male student uses the expression 'Sam, mate. I'm so *crunk*!'. While 'crunk' can easily be defined with a quick look at a slang dictionary (crazy + drunk, excited), Coleman points out that 'the meaning of "crunk" is less important than its interpersonal function. Because "crunk" tends to be used in the context of hip hop and rap music, it confirms that Jack likes and understands the music and the cultural trends that go along with it'. (Coleman 2012)

So, if language is being used to signal aspects of our identities and our desire to show affiliation towards, or distance from, other groups of people, it is important to think about how and why this is done. Language writer and TV presenter, Susie Dent, writing about what she calls 'tribes' (a term she uses to describe the social or occupational groups that many people belong to) explains that, 'Every sport, every profession, every group united by a single passion draws on a lexicon that is uniquely theirs, and theirs for a reason. These individual languages are the products of a group's needs, ambitions and personalities ...'. (Dent 2016)

Dent goes on to discuss the identity-forming (and identity-reinforcing) role of such sociolects and occupational registers (or forms of lingo, as she puts it): 'Whatever our reason for using it, our lingo is our identity. Whether it's the craic [Irish term for "humour"] of comedians or the verbal sidesteps of politicians, private languages are a loud marker of who we are or want to be, and where we fit (or don't) in society'. (Dent 2016)

Some forms of language will signal that we are part of a group, or wish to be seen as part of it (so-called in-group language), while at the same time keeping others out. The activities we are engaged in will inevitably have an impact on the language we use as part of the group as well as the nature of the group.

## 2.1.2 Discourse communities and communities of practice

Those who belong to particular groups – be they social or occupational – often belong to discourse communities. A discourse community is a group of people engaged in similar activities, usually work-based or around a specialist interest, who use language in distinct and identifiable ways.

John Swales (1990) defines a discourse community as having members who:

- have a shared set of common goals

- communicate internally, using one or more mechanisms and genres of communication

- use specialist vocabulary and discourse primarily to provide information and feedback

- have a required level of knowledge and expertise to be considered eligible to participate in the community.

Discourse communities use language for shared purposes and, as Swales puts it, 'In a discourse community, the communicative needs of the goals tend to predominate in the development and maintenance of its discoursal characteristics.' (Swales 1990)

The specialist lexis employed by many discourse communities makes communication much easier within the group – the shared terms and frames of reference allow the members to assume a certain degree of prior knowledge and understanding, for example – but can be confusing and opaque to outsiders. The term jargon is often applied to such technical or professional lexis, and the term sometimes carries connotations of disdain, implying that the language is sometimes deliberately obscure in order to prevent others understanding it. The Plain English Campaign sees such language as a barrier to understanding and since 1997 has 'been campaigning against gobbledygook, jargon and misleading public information'.

## KEY TERMS

**Discourse community:** a group of people with shared interests and belief systems who are likely to use language in similar ways

**Jargon:** the vocabulary and manner of speech that define and reflect a particular profession which may be difficult for others to understand

The media representation of the language of some occupational groups can be quite critical. Texts 2A and 2B are extracts from an article in The Huffington Post about workplace speech and an article on The Conversation website about business jargon.

### Text 2A

That's not to say that all jargon-users are liars; some well-meaning language-manglers are just trying to fit in with their contemporaries. But that doesn't make it excusable. The use of a vapid verbal shortcut is an attempt to convey a point without pausing to consider whether or not the correct point is being conveyed, or whether or not the point is worth conveying at all.

The promotion of thoughtless chatter is noxious enough, but contemporary workplace jargon isn't always just trite — it can also create an atmosphere of belligerence. Office speak can be aggressive, patriarchal and, when you really consider the language, remarkably unprofessional. *Killing it* and *bleeding edge* seem straight out of *American Psycho*, or at least a hyped-up workplace fueled by caffeine, testosterone and high fives. Offices (well, American offices, anyway) have long employed masculine ways of speaking, borrowed from sporty or militaristic language—consider *teamwork, give 110 percent* and *take it to the next level*. Or worse: *targeting clients with guerrilla marketing*.

Extract from Maddie Crum, 'Why Workplace Jargon is a Big Problem'
(*The Huffington Post*, 25 April 2014)

### Text 2B

During the past decade, surveys by pollsters, HR [Human Resources] agencies and academics have canvassed workers' views and identified the use of jargon as a major irritant. Junior executives and office workers in particular feel intimidated and excluded by superiors' obscure and pretentious language. They also suspect that this is often employed to conceal incompetence, or disguise unpalatable decisions.

The version of Chinese whispers through which such language spreads can result in embarrassing gaffes. *Across the piste*, a phrase inspired by skiing, became fashionable not long ago to mean something like 'taking the widest perspective' or 'affecting a wide range of people'. Through mishearing or misunderstanding, many professionals now say *across the piece*, while a hapless few are guilty of *across the beast*.

It is inevitable that technical language will cross over into everyday usage, when it deals with aspects of technology and commerce, for instance *big data, the internet of things, crowdfunding* and *clickbait*. This is also the case when language describes changes that are affecting our lives such as *negative equity, downturns* and *downsizing, outsourcing* and *offshoring*, or when it provides a shorthand for fairly complex concepts such as 'the glass ceiling', 'the precariat' or 'soft power'.

But the spread of management-speak and the language of the market into other spheres is not something neutral or innocent, as academic linguists working in the field of what's called critical discourse analysis have pointed out.

It carries with it the ideology – the values and assumptions – of market capitalism.

Extract from Tony Thorne, 'Translated: the baffling world of business jargon' (The Conversation, 29 January 2016)

## ACTIVITY 2.1
### Workplace jargon

Think about the ways in which these extracts present workplace language and try to pinpoint some of the language choices made by the writers. How do these choices help create a sense of workplace jargon as a problem to outsiders? What are the wider problems of using business jargon implied in the second text? What alternative arguments could you offer, in defence of some of the language used by people in different occupational groups?

What do you understand about the meanings of the jargon terms that have been used? Look up their meanings to find out more about them.

An alternative way of theorising about groups of people using language together is to see them as communities of practice. While the notion of discourse communities is one that derives from the discipline of linguistics (and is primarily concerned with language – hence *discourse* community rather than community of discourse), the originators of the ideas around communities of practice were the anthropologists Jean Lave and Etienne Wenger, so in their model the community of people comes first and the *practice* – for our purposes, the *linguistic* practice – comes second. Linguists such as Penelope Eckert and Sally McConnell-Ginet (1992) and Emma Moore (2010) have made use of the idea of communities of practice to explore how groups of people interact with each other to develop ways of making sense of what they are doing, ways of organising within the group and (probably most importantly from our perspective) ways of talking. As Eckert and McConnell-Ginet put it themselves:

> A community of practice is an aggregate of people who come together around mutual engagement in some common endeavor. Ways of doing things, ways of talking, beliefs, values, power relations – in short, practices – emerge in the course of their joint activity around that endeavor. A community of practice is different as a social construct from the traditional notion of community, primarily because it is defined simultaneously by its membership and by the practice in which that membership engages. Indeed, it is the practices of the community and members' differentiated participation in them that structures the community socially. (Eckert and McConnell-Ginet 1992)

> **KEY TERM**
>
> **Community of practice:** a group of people engaged in a shared activity or practice, whose language is shaped by the activities they are mutually engaged in

Moore's ethnographic study of teenage girls aged between 12 and 15 from Bolton in the north-west of England (2010) looks at four communities of practice: the Populars, the Townies, the Geeks and the Eden Valley Girls, all of whom come from a range of different social backgrounds but who differentiate themselves from other social groups. According to Sue Fox's account of the Eden Village Girls' study on the Linguistics Research Digest, Moore was able to observe a number of areas including:

> the girls' personal appearance and style, the people that each of them spent time with, the activities that they engaged in and the girls' attitudes to their own membership of groups and towards other groups. (Fox 2011)

By focusing on one linguistic variable – the use of the verb form *was* or *were* in a standard 'I was', or non-standard 'I were', construction – Moore noticed varying uses of the feature. Some were clearly linked to class and social background, particularly among the Eden Valley Girls who were all from a higher social class than the other groups, but in other cases it appeared that the nature of the group's identity might have been more important than the social class make-up of that group. What this might suggest is that while linguists have long known that many variables such as gender, region, age, class and ethnicity can have an influence on language use, the social practices of groups can sometimes be more important in shaping language identity.

# 2.2 Social class and language

The social context that we are born into is one key way in which we might be grouped. Social class as a concept is something that is notoriously difficult to define and consists of a number of factors including:

- type and level of education (state/private, university and post-16)

- family income

- cultural activities (music, theatre, computer games, opera, etc.)

- social circles and friendship groups.

Sociologist Fiona Devine and economist Mike Savage (Savage *et al*, 2013) identified seven social classes in the UK and the forms of 'capital' of each class from a survey they conducted in January 2011. Their findings (summarised in Table 2.1) were based on the responses of 160,000 people to the 'Great British Class Calculator' commissioned by the BBC.

Table 2.1: Adapted from the BBC's Great British Class Survey

| Class | Economic, cultural and/or social capital | Other characteristics |
|---|---|---|
| Elite | High levels of all three capitals | High economic capital distinguished them from all other classes |
| Established middle class | High levels of all three capitals but lower than the elite | Gregarious and culturally engaged |
| Technical middle class | High economic capital but less culturally and socially engaged | Small new class with few social contacts |
| New affluent workers | Medium levels of economic capital and higher levels of cultural and social capital | Young, active group |
| Emergent service workers | Low economic capital but high cultural and social capital | New class of young people, often in cities |
| Traditional working class | Low levels of all three capitals but higher economic capital than the precariat | Average age is older than in other classes |
| Precariat | Lowest levels of all three capitals | Members' everyday lives are precarious |

The link between language and social class is an interesting one and can itself be influenced by many other factors. A working class person from Leeds (in the north of England) will not necessarily use the same language features as a working class person from Oklahoma (in the USA), nor will a middle class person from East London speak like a middle class person from Dublin (in the Republic of Ireland). However, members of these social classes may share some characteristics of non-Standard English, compared to the often Standard English of upper class speakers.

The anthropologist Kate Fox, writing about language and class in her book, *Watching The English*, describes what she terms the different linguistic class codes which are often based on stereotypes of behaviour:

The first class indicator concerns which type of letter you favour in your pronunciation — or rather, which type you fail to pronounce. Those at the top of the social scale like to think that their way of speaking is 'correct', as it is clear and intelligible and accurate, while lower-class speech is 'incorrect', a lazy way of talking – unclear, often unintelligible, and just plain wrong. Exhibit A in this argument is the lower-class failure to pronounce consonants, in particular the glottal stop – the omission (swallowing, dropping) of 't's – and the dropping of 'h's.

But this is a case of the pot calling the kettle (or ke'le, if you prefer) black. The lower ranks may drop their consonants but the upper class are equally guilty of dropping their vowels. If you ask them the time, for example, the lower classes may tell you it is "alf past ten' but the upper class will say 'hpstn'. Handkerchief in working-class speech is "ankercheef', but in upper-class pronunciation becomes 'hnkrchf'. (Fox 2005)

Linguists are generally careful not to describe language using deficit models. As a non-linguist, Fox might be forgiven for describing language variation as 'lazy' or 'wrong', particularly when she is even-handed in her criticisms!

---

### KEY TERM

**Deficit model:** a way of describing a form of language as lacking, or deficient in, some quality – linguists tend to avoid such judgements

---

## 2.2.1 Researching language and class

Studies of language and social class often focus on accent as a marker of social identity and status, and foreground the differences between what are perceived to be working class (often regional) accents and Received Pronunciation (RP) which became established as the most socially prestigious accent in the UK in the early- to mid-Victorian period.

There is no doubt that some accents are perceived to be more 'posh' than others and for a long time RP has carried these connotations. There is nothing intrinsically better in one sound than another, but the social class and status connotations of some sounds have been established and reinforced in their use by those of an upper class background for many years. Interestingly, attitudes to RP vary, depending on who you ask, where they live and their own social class.

Writing about RP and the studies carried out by Howard Giles in the 1970s, Peter Trudgill notes that:

It was apparent from Giles' work that RP was perceived as being an accent associated, in the absence of information to the contrary, with speakers who were competent, reliable, educated, and confident. It was also perceived as being the most aesthetically pleasing of all British English accents. On the other hand, RP speakers scored low on traits like friendliness, companionability, and sincerity, and messages couched in RP also proved to be less persuasive than the same messages in local accents. (Notice also that there is a long history in American science-fiction and horror films for sinister, menacing characters to be given RP accents.) (Trudgill 2001)

A 2014 survey by the polling company YouGov (see Table 2.2) noted that RP was seen as attractive by 53 per cent of those surveyed in the UK, compared to 22 per cent who saw it as unattractive, but this varied according to the location, age, social class, political leanings and gender of the respondents.

## ACTIVITY 2.2
### Investigating attitudes

Think about a way to measure attitudes to different accents. Perhaps you could write a short script and ask friends with different accents – RP and a regional one – to read the script aloud. If you then record these and play them back to others, you can ask what the respondents like or dislike about each recording. Also think about the limitations of such a study and how you might devise a more developed methodology for a bigger project. Remember to be ethical in your research and seek the permission of the respondents to use their data.

# 2.2.2 Language up and down: convergence and divergence

It is these varying attitudes to RP that perhaps explain why some RP-speakers in positions of authority and power in the UK feel the need to change their accent when speaking to members of different social classes. In one infamous incident, former UK Chancellor of the Exchequer, Gideon 'George' Oliver Osborne (privately-educated son of a seventeenth baronet) was derided for dropping his RP accent and speaking 'mockney' (mock-Cockney, an accent associated with working or lower middle-class speakers from the south-east of England) to an audience of supermarket workers at a Morrisons warehouse. (The footage of Osborne's speech can be found here in a clip from ITN: www.cambridge.org/links/escdiv6011.) Sam Masters, writing for the Independent newspaper in 2013, described it as follows:

> The Old Etonian has previous when it comes to letting his normally immaculate and dainty received pronunciation slide for big speeches. But when he said he was 'findin savins' he was immediately subjected to

Table 2.2: YouGov survey results (2014). For each of the following accents, please say how attractive or unattractive you think they are…

Fieldwork: 27th – 28th November 2014

| | Total % | Gender | | Age | | | | Social grade | | Region | | | | |
| --- | --- | --- | --- | --- | --- | --- | --- | --- | --- | --- | --- | --- | --- | --- |
| | | Male % | Female % | 18-24 % | 25-39 % | 40-59 % | 60+ % | ABC1 % | C2DE % | London % | Rest of south % | Midlands/ Wales % | North % | Scotland % |
| **Cockney** | | | | | | | | | | | | | | |
| Very attractive | 3 | 3 | 4 | 3 | 2 | 4 | 4 | 3 | 3 | 8 | 3 | 3 | 2 | 2 |
| Fairly attractive | 22 | 18 | 26 | 15 | 22 | 20 | 28 | 22 | 22 | 23 | 27 | 22 | 16 | 19 |
| TOTAL ATTRACTIVE | 25 | 21 | 30 | 18 | 24 | 24 | 32 | 25 | 25 | 31 | 30 | 25 | 18 | 21 |
| Fairly unattractive | 30 | 28 | 32 | 27 | 29 | 30 | 31 | 32 | 27 | 32 | 28 | 29 | 29 | 37 |
| Very unattractive | 25 | 29 | 21 | 29 | 26 | 27 | 21 | 26 | 24 | 15 | 20 | 27 | 35 | 26 |
| TOTAL UNATTRACTIVE | 55 | 57 | 53 | 56 | 55 | 57 | 52 | 58 | 51 | 47 | 48 | 56 | 64 | 63 |
| Neither attractive nor unattractive | 15 | 16 | 13 | 15 | 13 | 17 | 13 | 14 | 16 | 13 | 17 | 13 | 14 | 11 |
| Don't know | 6 | 6 | 5 | 10 | 9 | 3 | 2 | 4 | 7 | 9 | 5 | 6 | 3 | 5 |
| **Received Pronunciation (BBC English)** | | | | | | | | | | | | | | |
| Very attractive | 14 | 13 | 14 | 11 | 13 | 14 | 15 | 16 | 11 | 24 | 17 | 8 | 11 | 8 |
| Fairly attractive | 39 | 36 | 41 | 41 | 36 | 38 | 41 | 43 | 34 | 37 | 41 | 41 | 36 | 32 |
| TOTAL ATTRACTIVE | 53 | 49 | 55 | 52 | 49 | 52 | 56 | 59 | 45 | 61 | 58 | 49 | 47 | 40 |
| Fairly unattractive | 14 | 15 | 13 | 9 | 18 | 13 | 13 | 13 | 16 | 11 | 12 | 18 | 13 | 21 |
| Very unattractive | 8 | 9 | 6 | 9 | 7 | 7 | 9 | 5 | 11 | 5 | 6 | 8 | 12 | 9 |
| TOTAL UNATTRACTIVE | 22 | 24 | 19 | 18 | 25 | 20 | 22 | 18 | 27 | 16 | 18 | 26 | 25 | 30 |
| Neither attractive nor unattractive | 19 | 19 | 19 | 19 | 16 | 23 | 18 | 19 | 19 | 15 | 19 | 16 | 24 | 22 |
| Don't know | 6 | 7 | 6 | 10 | 10 | 5 | 4 | 4 | 9 | 8 | 5 | 8 | 5 | 8 |

ridicule. He was accused of adopting Tony Blair's often calculated use of Estuarine English [Estuary English is a dialect of UK English used around the Thames Estuary] and 'sounding like a chav' as he freely littered his spending round statement with 'wannas, lemmes' and 'gonnas'.
(Masters 2013)

What Osborne demonstrates in this clip is an example of downwards convergence, a form of linguistic accommodation. Accommodation explains the ways in which people vary their linguistic styles (including accents) to move closer towards or further from their interlocutors or perceived target audiences. In Osborne's case, the shift he makes is from a prestigious variety to one seen as lower class. Why does he do it? Only Osborne himself could genuinely answer this, but one linguistic reason might be that the public perceptions of RP are as upper class and prestigious, but rather distant. By shifting to a more working class accent, he might be hoping to gain some of the warmer and more relatable qualities of working class speech.

Movements can also take place in the opposite direction (upwards convergence) and might be found in situations where it is felt that a more sophisticated or formal style (or even posher accent) might be required. Think about times when you might have used either of these forms of convergence and why you did it. Divergence is another aspect of accommodation theory and describes the process of moving speech style away from others. This can signal a desire to maintain social distance from others or be used to exaggerate individual speech characteristics and mark oneself as different in some way, or perhaps proud of a separate identity.

## KEY TERMS

**Downwards convergence:** a speaker's emphasis on the non-standard aspects of their speech emphasising the covert prestige of non-standard forms

**Accommodation:** how people adjust their speech behaviours to match others; this can be aspects of accent, grammar, vocabulary and even the style of speech delivery

**Upwards convergence:** a speaker's emphasis on the standard aspects of their speech emphasising the prestige of standard forms

**Divergence:** when an individual changes their language choices (usually temporarily) to become more dissimilar to another individual or group

**RESEARCH QUESTION**

**Social and regional variations in the UK**

Use the British Library Sounds Familiar? website to explore and listen to some of the sounds of different social and regional variations in the UK. The section on RP is particularly helpful for explaining the difference between some of the sounds used in social varieties of UK English: www.cambridge.org/links/escdiv6012.

## 2.2.3 Codes: restricted and elaborated

Some of the first writing about language and social class was by the sociologist Basil Bernstein in the late 1960s and early 1970s. He argued that two codes of language existed – restricted and elaborated – and that these codes were used for different functions and by different social classes. While his work has been looked at critically by many linguists since then, his ideas are useful to introduce here. The restricted code tended to use simple grammatical constructions, co-ordination of clauses, more concrete and context-dependent vocabulary, thus relying on an understanding of the situation to make complete sense. Elaborated code had more complex grammatical constructions (in the form of greater use of subordinating conjunctions such as *because* and *if*, for example) and a more abstract vocabulary (more abstract nouns/noun phrases), allowing more chance to theorise and to extrapolate than the restricted code which would generally feature more concrete nouns. The codes were not exclusive to certain social classes but tended to be used differently by those in different occupations (a key factor in classifying social class). Class, therefore, did not necessarily determine the language being used by individuals, but by nature of the very occupations and activities carried out in different classes, had an influence.

## 2.2.4 Class, groups and social networks

Particular linguistic variables such as how /h/ sounds are produced, or whether an /-in/ or /-iŋ/ ending is used on words such as 'raining' or 'singing', can also be interesting to focus on and tell us something about the links between social class and language use, as well as perceptions of language use.

Peter Trudgill's 1968 study of the -iŋ/-in variable in Norwich suggested that the sound was produced differently depending on the social class the speaker belonged to (with much more use of the non-standard, regional -in form among the lower working class than middle-class speakers) but that other factors were important too. The nature of the context – whether it was casual conversation, or being asked to read word lists – along with the gender of the respondent (more males than females using the non-standard -*in* form) were also important, showing that while class is clearly a factor in language use, it is part of a wider range of variables.

Malcolm Petyt's 1985 study of h-dropping (not pronouncing the /h/ sound at the start of words such as 'hat' or 'house') showed a similar link between class and a linguistic variable associated with non-standard pronunciation (see Figure 2.1).

Figure 2.1: /h/-dropping in Norwich and West Yorkshire social groups

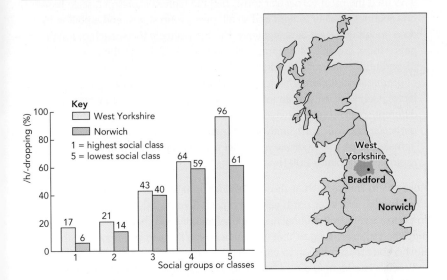

A sense of belonging to a group can also be a major factor in how people use language. The work of Milroy and Milroy in the north of Ireland (1978) identified what they termed social networks and their importance to language use. Networks are patterns of connections that individuals have to others in their community and beyond.

> The more tightly knit the network structure, and the more integrated an individual is into the group, the stronger the impetus to adhere to the group's accepted norms of behaviour. In Western societies strong tight-knit networks can be found in traditional 'working-class' communities. People tend to live, work and socialise in a compact setting. More middle-class communities tend to be characterised by looser network structures, with greater mobility for work, leisure and housing. Strong networks promote the maintenance of local linguistic features while looser networks are conduits for linguistic change. (Foulkes and Docherty 2007)

So, along with membership of a particular social class, a person's connections to others within that class and those outside it have a clear influence on how language might be used, whether it is the pronunciation of a specific sound, use of a lexical item (a word or phrase), or a grammatical structure. In her Reading study (1982), Jenny Cheshire identified a range of vernacular (non-standard) features, such as multiple negation ('I never did nothing') or non-standard past tense ('I come down here yesterday') that were used by the teenagers she was studying. She found that differences were at least partly down to the social groups the young people were part of, but also their gender.

> Overall boys used vernacular forms more frequently than girls did. The boys who used the most vernacular forms had the highest score on a scale based on toughness (ability to fight and steal), peer group status, and ambition to do a 'tough' job such as slaughterer. But interestingly the speech of tough girls – those capable of swearing, stealing or setting fire to the adventure playground – was quite distinguishable from that of the boys on a number of grammatical features. So toughness was here not the distinguishing factor. Gender itself was an influential explanatory factor accounting for different speech patterns which were observed. In these communities, particular linguistic forms may signal membership of the group 'male' or 'female' rather than indicate a speaker's social class background or social aspirations. (Holmes 2001)

More recent studies such as those in Middlesbrough (Llamas 2000) and Berwick-upon-Tweed, in the far north-east of England (Llamas 2006), which focus on people's sense of national and regional identity and their use of particular linguistic variables, suggest that while *where* you live can be important, the sense of who you are, in relation to your peers, your regional and national background and social class identity are all key factors in language use too. In the words of Ian Brown, singer of the influential 1990s Manchester band, The Stone Roses, 'It's not where you're from; it's where you're at'.

# 2.3 Parallel lives: slang and occupational English

When groups of people get together, language is used in different ways: generally, to communicate ideas from one to another and to perform social roles. The language itself is also shaped by the nature of the group and what develops is often influenced by the ways in which the individuals in the group interact and the contexts they operate within. For example, a group of soldiers working in close proximity to each other in a hostile environment are likely to build up a shared set of reference points based on their relationships and duties, and are also likely to have some quite specialised lexis to refer to the tools of their trade. This is the same within any occupational group, be it plumbers, care workers, lawyers or dentists. At the same time, while the vocabulary is a fairly obvious feature of many groups' language, other elements contribute to their shared repertoire.

---

## KEY TERM

**Repertoire:** a range of language features available for speakers to choose from

---

In the military, there are certain expectations about the nature of interactions that take place between different ranks, so the rules of turn-taking and interaction are different from those that exist outside the armed forces. This might link to the nature of some of the grammatical constructions, where orders are likely to be imperative in form (and commanding in function).

---

## ACTIVITY 2.3
### Occupational English

Think about three or four occupational groups that you have come across, either through family connections, your own experience or some other knowledge of their work. What are the characteristic features of the language used by these groups and how would you categorise these features into different areas such as their vocabulary and interactional styles?

---

These ideas link back to the work earlier in this chapter on discourse communities. The armed forces are a good example of how a discourse community operates, matching the key descriptors that Swales suggested (section 2.1.2).

Alongside the specialist, occupational language used within this group, other forms of language might also arise. As Coleman points out in *The Life of Slang* (2012), the conditions within the military are a perfect breeding ground for slang as well.

Slang is a form of language that many people will recognise but few will be able to define very clearly. The *Oxford English Dictionary* provides a number of definitions, but the two most relevant for the focus here are:

1b: The special vocabulary or phraseology of a particular calling or profession; the cant or jargon of a certain class or period.

1c: Language of a highly colloquial type, considered as below the level of standard educated speech, and consisting either of new words or of current words employed in some special sense.

Here, the overlap between occupational language and the very informal language of particular social groups is a little muddied. In recent years, the latter definition (1c) has tended to be the more popular way of defining slang, and it is clear from this definition that part of what makes slang 'slang' is its informality and 'lower level' communication. Slang therefore seems to be something quite different from the occupational lexis described earlier, fulfilling a different set of functions. If occupational language is all about doing the job and using language to do that job effectively and smoothly, then slang is an expression of how you feel about your job and how you wish to present yourself as an individual within that group. It runs parallel to the occupational discourse but underneath it, in terms of its formality and appropriacy.

In the case of the military, Coleman points out that a compelling set of conditions exists for the creation and diffusion of slang:

- A heightened desire for self-expression ('Where all individuality is stripped away by uniforms, regulation haircuts and the necessity of obeying orders without question, the desire to identify oneself as a separate human being becomes problematic.')

- Slang speakers are lower in the hierarchy ('In a military setting, all behavior that is potentially threatening to the hierarchy is carefully monitored, and infringements of the rules are sometimes brutally punished, but slang offers the possibility for minor rebellion that won't usually meet with serious consequences.')

- A sense of group identity ('Living under shared circumstances of inferiority and uniformity, individuals will use slang among themselves to heighten their sense of solidarity.')

- A sense that their position is unfair or unreasonable ('Oppressed groups at the bottom of hierarchies are denied their individuality in many settings, but the conditions for slang development are best where individuals collectively resist the forces acting upon them by means short of physical violence.') (Quotations from Coleman 2012)

It is not just the military where slang thrives. If most of the conditions outlined above are met in different settings, slang can develop. Prisoners, boarding school pupils, criminal gangs, doctors and journalists all develop their own slangs, as do many other groups, occupational or otherwise. Such slang is often completely alien to outsiders and for good reason. If the general public heard how some doctors referred to some of their patients in less than flattering terms they might be horrified. For example, 'Crinkly' = a geriatric, elderly patient, 'Frequent Flyer' = someone who is well known to doctors as being in hospital for dubious reasons, 'Blue Bloater' = an obese person suffering respiratory failure, or 'FLK' = Funny Looking Kid. However, there are many terms equally critical of others within the profession, so in some respects this kind of slang is equal opportunities in its targets.

Youth slang is one area that has often attracted considerable interest outside linguistic circles, because of its constantly changing nature. As a social group, young people are clearly very varied, with many sub-groups within the broader group, but some patterns of age-related language use can still be seen.

Figure 2.2: Relationship between age and use of 'prestige' forms

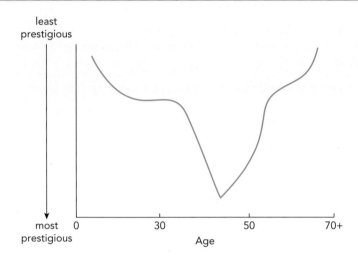

In Figure 2.2, the graph would suggest that young people are the main users of vernacular forms of language, that their speech becomes more standard as they approach adulthood and middle age, before it tails off and becomes non-standard again as they approach later life.

There is something inevitable in younger generations developing their own way of talking and writing, because it is something that has happened for centuries, and the desire to create a new identity – separate from parents and their lifestyles and values – is a natural stage of adolescent development. As we have seen in this chapter, language does so much more than communicate transactional information, so it is hardly surprising that it can be used by young people to signal their membership of a different age group and delineate their territory against that of their parents.

## ACTIVITY 2.4

### Teenage outrage

Examine the headlines in Text 2C, which are taken from a range of different articles from the Mail Online, a UK newspaper, reporting on teenage slang. What are the main patterns that you notice in the descriptions of this language and the users of it?

**Text 2C**

'It's thug life innit': Confused parents confess they are baffled by the language their teenage sons use

'"Snow" is drugs and "salad" equals sex: Do you have any idea what the words in your teenagers' texts mean?'

PIR (Parent In Room), IPN (I'm Posting Naked) and WTTP (Want To Trade Photos): The 28 internet acronyms EVERY parent needs to look out for

Don't let your kids GNOC! Parents warned about teen sexting codes

The teens who can barely talk – they only have an 800-word vocabulary

Figure 2.3: Good advice for teenagers?

---

**TEENAGERS**

Tired of being

harassed by

your parents?

**ACT NOW!**

Move out, get a job,

& pay your own way.

**QUICK!**

While you still

know everything!

---

## PRACTICE QUESTION
### The influence of social groups on use of language
Discuss the idea that the social groups people belong to have an influence on the ways in which they use language.

# Wider reading

You can find out more about the topics in this chapter by reading the following:

## Diversity and language

Holmes, J. and Wilson, N. (2017) *An Introduction to Sociolinguistics* (Fifth edition). London: Routledge.

## Language used by different social groups

Coleman, J. (2012) *The Life of Slang*. Oxford: Oxford University Press.

Dent, S. (2016) *Modern Tribes: The Secret Languages of Britain*. London: John Murray.

# Chapter 3
## Ethnicity

In this chapter you will:

- Consider what is meant by 'ethnicity'
- Explore some existing and current research on the relationship between ethnicity and language
- Investigate media representations of language and ethnicity

Ethnicity and language have a fascinating, although often very complex, relationship. In some ways, it's quite easy to imagine how somebody's ethnic background will have an effect on how they use English. For example, if somebody migrated to an English-speaking country with English as their second language, then it would be no surprise that their first language would influence the way they speak. However, the situation is less clear when we consider the children, grandchildren and great-grandchildren of these same people. Second- and third-generation migrants will usually have English as a first language, yet it is often not quite the same variety of English as the local 'native speakers' (you will consider the term 'native speakers' more in Chapter 4). Things start getting even more complicated when there are multiple linguistic influences at work, as urban centres around the world become more and more culturally diverse, and young people grow up exposed to many language varieties. In this chapter you will explore some of these themes, and begin to understand how our ethnicities are in many ways another aspect of our identities that we construct and perform through our use of language.

## KEY TERM

**Ethnicity:** a shared social identity consisting of cultural practices, language, beliefs and history. You have some control over your ethnic affiliation

# 3.1 Race and ethnicity

Race and ethnicity are two terms which are often confused or used interchangeably. In the past, the difference between the two might have been seen in the same way as the difference between sex and gender: one is biological and the other is socially constructed. However, the situation is not so simple. It turns out that it is not actually possible to classify all human beings into definitive racial categories on the basis of biology after all. These days, race and ethnicity are both understood as social constructs. This doesn't mean that they are not real, it just means that they are as much to do with perception (and self-identity) as they are to do with objective, measurable facts.

Race is still seen as having a connection to biology, relating as it does to perceived shared physical characteristics. Ethnicity, on the other hand, relates to shared cultural practices and beliefs. This definition from Lawrence Bobo is useful:

> Common usage tends to associate 'race' with biologically based differences between human groups, differences typically observable in skin color, hair

texture, eye shape, and other physical attributes. 'Ethnicity' tends to be associated with culture, pertaining to such factors as language, religion, and nationality. (Bobo 2001)

The fact is, it is very difficult to pin down a stable meaning for either term, as they both depend on the context of use and what happens to be socially significant in that context at that time. There is also a large role to be played by self-identification (that is, how you view your own race or ethnicity), especially in situations of mixed heritage.

At the time of writing this chapter, a news article emerged which perfectly illustrates the social nature of race. The article, written by Arwa Mahdawi (2017), discusses possible changes to the US census which would add a 'Middle East/ North Africa' category, a category that didn't exist previously. People who match this description currently fall into the category 'White'. The proposed changes will essentially alter people's race, at least according to how they are viewed by government agencies. The story points out other instances of 'whiteness' being a fluid concept with historical examples of movement in the other direction, such as Irish Americans, Italian Americans and Jews. What really defines whiteness, Mahdawi argues, is not melanin or nationality, but power.

## KEY TERM

**Race:** perceived physical similarities and differences that groups and cultures consider socially significant. You generally cannot choose your race

## ACTIVITY 3.1
### Your race and ethnicity

How do you describe yourself in terms of race and/or ethnicity? Is it something you find easy to do, or can it be difficult? Have you ever been described by someone else in a different way from how you perceive yourself? What do you think are the most important factors that play a role in determining a person's ethnicity?

Compare the official ethnicity categories from the UK (e.g. www.cambridge.org/links/escdiv6013) and the USA (e.g. www.cambridge.org/links/escdiv6014). How do they differ? Would you have to define yourself differently in each country, or are you the same in both? Now find the official categories from somewhere else. Are there any differences?

# 3.2 Heritage language

In many cases an important influence on the way we speak English is what's known as our heritage language. A typical situation in the UK would be where a teenager of Indian heritage has English as a first language, but the main language in the family home is Punjabi. At school and with friends this teenager is likely to use English, but at home is likely to use a mixture of English and Punjabi.

> **KEY TERM**
>
> **Heritage language:** a language that is not the dominant language in the society in which somebody lives, yet it is one that is spoken at home

In such situations it is often the case that each generation has a very different relationship with both the heritage language (Punjabi) and the dominant language (English) due to their different experiences, choices and expectations. For example, an Indian couple starting a new life in Britain in the 1960s (our present-day teenager's grandparents) would have likely been keen to learn the language and attempt to assimilate into the local culture. However, their first language would have had a great influence on the way they used English. This couple's children would then have been brought up in 1970s and 80s Britain – a time of hostility towards migrants, when it was perhaps even more desirable to fit in socially and linguistically. This would have led to an increased pressure to use English, and maybe a rejection of Punjabi and the associated cultural practices so familiar to their parents. At the same time, the original couple might have now brought *their* parents over to Britain (our teenager's great-grandparents), who are likely to have had no English, and limited opportunity or desire to learn any.

Figure 3.1: Different generations will have different relationships with the heritage language

When the next generation is born, in the 1990s and 2000s (our teenager), things were very different. Hostility towards migrants had reduced, and people were used to living in a much more ethnically mixed society. This is a particularly interesting generation, as there are several possible influences on the way they might speak. On the one hand, they are growing up in the same English-dominant environment as their parents, so will be using English as a first language. On the other hand, the variety of English they are being exposed to is quite different from that of 40 years ago. As you will see later in this chapter, the English of twenty first-century urban Britain is itself influenced by various additional languages, some of which can in fact be traced back to the heritage language in question! In addition to this, the accepted diversity of their immediate environment might now encourage a renewed sense of identification with their ethnicity and heritage language.

As you can see, the situation is complicated. Each generation experiences different types of social, linguistic and cultural influences and interactions, and each has a different relationship with the heritage language. When we then consider the intersectionality between ethnicity and other important social factors such as class and gender, things start getting even more interesting. The result of all this is a great deal of variation even among people who share an ethnicity. However, there are also some similarities, which you will explore a little bit later.

### KEY TERM

**Intersectionality:** the idea that social categorisations are all interconnected and overlapping. Someone's ethnicity cannot be separate from their gender, social class, sexuality, and so on

# 3.3 Code-switching

When people routinely use more than one language in their everyday lives, they will often find themselves code-switching to some extent. This refers to the process of switching from one language (code) to another in mid-conversation, or even in mid-sentence. This is more than simply using one language with one group of people (family) and a different language with another group of people (friends and teachers), as the receivers must also be bilingual.

Code-switching can also occur among monolingual speakers, especially if there are two clear varieties available to be used (perhaps a strong regional or ethnic dialect and a more standard variety), but movement within the same language is often referred to as style-shifting.

## KEY TERMS

**Code-switching:** when speakers who speak two or more different languages switch from one to the other, often in mid-conversation depending on who they are talking to or what they wish to accomplish. Can also be used to refer to switching between dialects in the same language

**Style-shifting:** when speakers adjust the way they speak depending on a combination of factors such as how much attention they are paying to what they are saying, who they are talking to, or how they want to be perceived in a particular context

There can be lots of reasons to code-switch, but the reason that is relevant here is that one of its possible functions is the performance of ethnic identity. In her well-known book *An Introduction to Sociolinguistics*, Janet Holmes describes several examples of this kind of switching. She makes the point that speakers don't actually need to be proficient speakers of the second language to still make use of particular words and phrases that signal and reaffirm their ethnic identity to others, thus creating a sense of solidarity. One of her examples (Holmes 2013) takes place in a Maori/English context (Text 3A), when a newcomer to the conversation arrives and the greeting exchange takes place in Maori, consolidating the speakers' shared identity:

### Text 3A

[*The Maori is in italics.* THE TRANSLATION IS IN SMALL CAPITALS]

Sarah:     I think everyone's here except Mere.

John:      She said she might be a bit late but actually I think that's her arriving now.

Sarah:     You're right. *Kia ora Mere. Haere mai. Kei te pehea koe?*

           [HI MERE.     COME IN.     HOW ARE YOU?]

Mere:      *Kia ora e hoa. Kei te pai.* Have you started yet?

           [HELLO MY FRIEND. I'M FINE]

Extract from Holmes and Wilson, *An Introduction to Sociolinguistics* (Routledge, 2017)

Some bilinguals talk of almost having different identities in their different languages, and so switching is a way of performing one or other identity in a particular context. This is not to say that they are two different people, simply that there are certain moods or attitudes that are better suited to be expressed in a particular language, even if they have the ability to use either. Often these identities are related to the ethnicities and cultural practices each language is associated with.

## ACTIVITY 3.2
### Code-switching and style-shifting

If you have access to bilingual speakers, look at parts a and b below. If you don't have access to bilingual speakers, look at part b.

a) Do you regularly speak more than one language? Are you aware of code-switching yourself? Next time you are in a bilingual situation, try to keep track of when you or the people you are speaking to switch into each language. If you are with friends or family you might want to ask if they mind being recorded (you must always get permission before you record someone). Listen to everyone's speech and try to identify possible reasons for any switches. When you have done this, write down some of the examples and ask the speakers why they think they switched at these points. Do their reasons match yours?

b) US comedians Keegan-Michael Key and Jordan Peele are well known for their sketches around code-switching and style-shifting, particularly in relation to African American English and 'white' Standard English. Some sketches refer to Barack Obama's ability to seamlessly adjust his language according to his audience. Watch the two videos below and for each one make a note of which features (maybe words, grammatical structures, or pronunciations) indicate each style of speaking.

Key and Peele: 'Phone call'. www.cambridge.org/links/escdiv6015

Key and Peele: 'Obama meet and greet'. www.cambridge.org/links/escdiv6016

# 3.4 Accent and dialect variation

Whilst code-switching usually involves the use of words, phrases or grammatical structure from a different language as a means of performing ethnic identity (among other things), our ethnicity can also be expressed through the way in which we use English. This can be especially obvious of course in our accents.

People often think that we don't have much control over our accents in a second language, that it is simply a case of how proficient we are. But this is only true to a certain extent. It is generally accepted that the earlier we learn the second language, the more 'native-like' our pronunciation is likely to be (although there is little definitive evidence for a particular cut-off point), but at any age there is still a degree of individual agency over the way we sound.

Rob Drummond carried out a study (Drummond 2012, summarised here: www.cambridge.org/links/escdiv6017) in which he looked at the English pronunciation of Polish people living in Manchester. His main focus was to investigate the extent to which they acquired features of a Manchester accent, and to look at some of the social factors which might influence this. However, in the course of his research into the pronunciation of -ing in words such as 'feeling', 'swimming', and 'living' for example, he found something he wasn't expecting. In addition to the predictable variants of -ing/-ɪŋ/ and -in/-ɪn/ he also found quite a few people using -ink/-ɪŋk/. This wasn't surprising in itself, as it was clearly a Polish-influenced pronunciation (in Polish, the /ɪŋ/ sound can only occur before a /k/ or a /g/), but what was surprising was that there was no relationship between the use of this variant and an individual's level of English. In other words, the -inK pronunciation wasn't just being used because individual speakers hadn't mastered the local pronunciation, so there must be some other reason.

That reason turned out to be related to people's future plans. One of the questions people were asked related to what they intended to do in the future. Did they plan to stay in the UK or return to Poland? People who intended to return to Poland were more likely to use the -inK pronunciation, and less likely to use the -in pronunciation (this is the most common non-standard variant among British native English speakers). Because some of these speakers had very good English, Drummond interpreted this finding as an example of individuals using this pronunciation more or less consciously in order to signal some kind of allegiance or solidarity with their Polish ethnicity. In other words, they were very likely able to produce a more native-like pronunciation of -ing, but this was a small way in which they could perform their ethnic identity.

This part of Drummond's study was quantitative, which means he was mainly interested in counting how many times particular variants were used overall, and how these frequencies related to other measurable social factors shared between groups of speakers. While this can give interesting insights into general patterns, it does not tell anything about how a particular individual might be using their speech to perform aspects of their identity that relate to ethnicity, especially if the individual does different things with different people. This is something that Devyani Sharma has been able to show through her work looking at Punjabi-speaking Indians in West London (e.g. Sharma 2011).

Recognising that gathering speech data of this kind by way of an interview can be rather limiting (interviews and related tasks are a common way to collect data in sociolinguistic studies), Sharma and her colleagues asked their participants to record themselves as they went about their day-to-day lives, talking to different people. They then analysed the recordings, listening out for specific features which have a 'British' or 'Indian' variant, noting in which contexts they occurred. The features they focused on are in Table 3.1.

Table 3.1: Features used by Sharma (2011) in her study on Punjabi-speaking Indians in West London

| Feature | Indian variant | British variant |
|---|---|---|
| /t/ | Retroflex /t/. The tip of the tongue is curled upwards (or slightly backwards) and is placed further back on the roof of the mouth than a 'standard' British /t/ | Alveolar /t/. A standard British English /t/, with the tongue touching the alveolar ridge. The category also included a glottal stop /ʔ/ for this study. |
| FACE | The vowel in words such as 'place', 'main' and 'cake' is pronounced as a monophthong rather than a diphthong. | The vowel in these words is pronounced as a diphthong. |
| GOAT | The vowel in words such as 'go', 'boat' and 'know' is pronounced as a monophthong rather than a diphthong. | The vowel in these words is pronounced as a diphthong. |
| /l/ | Light /l/ The /l/ sound at the end of a syllable in words such as 'milk', 'feel', and 'pull' is *clear* rather than *dark*. Only the tip of the tongue is in contact with the roof of the mouth. This is the same as the standard British /l/ in words such as 'like'. | Dark /l/ The /l/ sound in these words is *dark* rather than *clear*. More of the tongue is in contact with the roof of the mouth and the back of the tongue is raised. |

## KEY TERMS

**Alveolar ridge:** the hard area behind the top front teeth

**Diphthong:** a vowel which starts as one sound then changes to another. For example, the /ɔɪ/ vowel sound in the word 'choice'

Sharma was able to show how individual speakers altered the frequency of Indian and British variants depending on who they were speaking to. One of the most extreme examples was a speaker named Anwar, a 41-year-old man.

He showed a great deal of variation in speech styles, from almost 100 per cent 'Indian' when speaking to a Sri-Lankan maid to 100 per cent 'British' when speaking to a mechanic, who Sharma describes as 'cockney' (a traditional working-class Londoner from the East End of the city), with various contexts in between. Figure 3.2 shows these two extremes and an additional intermediate context – speaking to an Asian school friend. The blue bars represent Indian variants and the yellow bars represent British variants. Anwar is a good example of the type of speaker mentioned earlier – someone who perhaps felt the need to be able to adapt socially and linguistically in order to fit into a society that was often hostile to immigrants. Through language, Anwar is able to perform both his Indian and his British identities depending on the perceived demands of the context. Sharma found that the younger speakers did not adjust their speech so much, arguing that there is perhaps less need to do so due to the different social environment in which they have grown up.

Figure 3.2: Use by older man (Anwar) of Indian and British variants across speaking situations. Adapted from Sharma (2011).

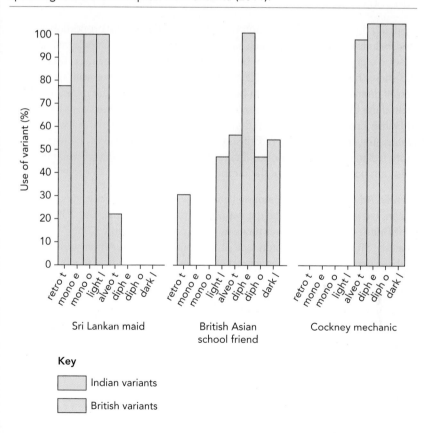

Key
Indian variants
British variants

In a follow-up study, Sharma and her colleague Ben Rampton (2015) looked in more depth at the ways in which individuals not only adjust their language between contexts depending on who they are speaking to, but also how they adjust their language within the same conversation, depending on the topic. This time, instead of counting the number of Indian or British variants within a conversation, they measured the number of variants within each segment of an interaction (the segments were divided along clausal boundaries). They looked at ten different speech features, most of which had three variants that could be described as Indian English (IndE), Standard British English (SBrE), and Vernacular British English (VBrE). They then counted how many of each variant occurred in a segment of the conversation.

For example, in the sentence 'After I went into the V and A, Victoria and Albert museum' they would identify those speech features which might be pronounced differently, such as the 't' and 'l' sounds (see Table 3.1), and decide whether the IndE, SBrE or VBrE variant was being used. Then they calculated the proportion of each in the segment as a whole – for example, 43% IndE, 27% SBrE, 30% VBrE.

By doing this, Sharma and Rampton were able to identify the proportion of British/Indian English across each stage of the conversation. Once again, Anwar showed a great deal of variation, but this time within the same interaction. Figure 3.3 shows how Anwar's speech fluctuated during a conversation with Devyani herself during an interview, when he was describing a visit to the museum. The main thing to look at here is the solid line, which represents the proportion of British English variants within that particular segment. When it is high, this means Anwar was using more British variants, and when it is low, he was using more Indian variants. The dotted line represents British vernacular variants, but these are not so important at the moment.

Clearly, Anwar shifted continuously between sounding more British and more Indian, but why should this be the case? Why did he sometimes use 100 per cent British variants and other times use 100 per cent Indian variants? In their analysis, Sharma and Rampton look at the content of what Anwar was saying at these particular points. The extract in Figure 3.3 represents a section of the conversation in which Anwar was recounting Britain's role in the turmoil of India's past, before expressing his dismay at the injustice of British museums displaying what could be seen as stolen artefacts. They found that the peaks of Indian variants occurred at times when Anwar was expressing 'personal or political outrage', or 'cultural insult'. In other words, Anwar was using particular linguistic features as a tool to align himself with particular ethnic and cultural viewpoints and identities.

Figure 3.3: 'Museum Visit' narrative, showing how Anwar used British English or Indian English variants depending on the content of what he was saying (adapted from Sharma and Rampton 2015)

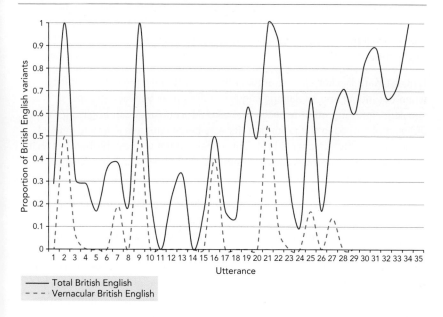

———— Total British English
– – – Vernacular British English

# 3.5 Ethnolect

Although the term ethnolect is intended to refer to any variety related to any ethnic group, more often than not, it is used in relation to an immigrant or minority population within a dominant white context. This imbalance leads many people to be uncomfortable with the term, as it can be seen to maintain a divide between the marked and marginalised ethnic minorities and the unmarked dominant population.

## KEY TERMS

**Ethnolect:** a variety of language that is associated with a particular ethnic group

**Marked:** something that stands out and is noticed as different from the norm

**Unmarked:** the common, regular, normal version of something that can go unnoticed

# Language Diversity and World Englishes

Linguist Penny Eckert makes the point that in the United States (where she does most of her work) 'the white Anglo variety is considered a regional dialect, while African American and Latino varieties are considered ethnic dialects' (Eckert 2008). In other words, white varieties of English can be categorised into various regional dialects, but non-white varieties tend to be bundled together as ethnolects, ignoring any possible regional variation they might show.

Linguist Kara Becker agrees, arguing that too often we prioritise ethnicity when describing and explaining linguistic differences between groups of speakers, ignoring other aspects. She uses African American English (AAE) as an example, making the point that 'its very name captures a variety defined by ethnic identity' (Becker 2014). This is despite the well-established fact that not all African Americans use AAE and not all AAE speakers are African American.

One of the things that people like Penny Eckert, Kara Becker and many others are arguing against is the fixed and static nature of ethnolects. Individuals are often seen as either being speakers or non-speakers of a particular ethnolect, which in turn helps fix their ethnic identity as something permanent. In reality, both speech varieties and ethnicities are a lot more fluid. It doesn't make sense to think of an ethnolect as a separate and distinct way of speaking, especially when we consider what exactly it is that makes one ethnolect different from another (or different from a mainstream dialect). The fact is, there are far more shared features between any two varieties of English than there are differences, just as there are far more similarities between people of different ethnicities.

What is needed then is a more helpful way of looking at ethnolects, and one option is the notion of ethnolinguistic repertoire. An ethnolinguistic repertoire is 'a fluid set of linguistic resources that members of an ethnic group may use variably as they index their ethnic identities' (Benor 2010) (here the word 'index' means something close to 'signal' or 'indicate'). An ethnolinguistic repertoire approach would look at how particular linguistic features are used (or not used) within social interaction in order to perform an individual's ethnic identity. The example used earlier of Sharma and Rampton's analysis of Anwar's speech is a good illustration of a repertoire approach in action.

## KEY TERM

**Ethnolinguistic repertoire:** a set of linguistic resources that are available to be used by individual speakers in order to signal their ethnic identity

All this doesn't mean that you shouldn't talk about ethnolects; the term is established and used widely. It simply means that when we do use the word ethnolect, we should be aware that in some ways we are imposing a sense of stability and fixedness on something that is actually much more fluid.

## 3.5.1 Multiethnolect

An alternative word that has been growing in usage recently is multiethnolect. It is a term that has been used to describe a variety of related phenomena in the language of modern urban contexts, especially in Europe. It highlights the mixed nature of our societies and the multiple influences on language. Cheshire et al (2015) describe some of the language forms and practices that might come under the term multiethnolect. The main ones are listed below.

- It refers to the way that in mixed multicultural neighbourhoods, young people may combine elements from different heritage languages with the dominant mainstream language.

- It describes a speech repertoire, consisting of an identifiable core of innovative features (see Multicultural London English below).

- It refers to a stylistic resource that people can use in certain contexts with certain speakers in a process of constructing identity.

> **KEY TERM**
>
> **Multiethnolect:** a collection of linguistic resources combining features from a variety of languages within a multi-ethnic, multicultural context

As with 'ethnolect', not everybody is happy with the term 'multiethnolect'. One of the problems is that it still prioritises ethnicity over and above other social factors in relation to our language. Another is that it fails to capture the fluidity of these ways of speaking, perhaps making it no less fixed than an ethnolect. However, there are no alternatives that everybody agrees on, so linguists tend to use the term that they feel most accurately describes what they are looking at. Again, this doesn't mean that you shouldn't use the term, it simply means that you should be aware of its possible limitations.

Despite these limitations, one particularly interesting aspect of multiethnolects is that by coming about as the result of a mixing of languages, ethnicities and cultures, they can actually be seen as ethnically neutral. A multiethnolect does not 'belong' to people from any one ethnic group – it is available to be used by anybody, including people from the monolingual 'host' community. This is especially evident in a multiethnolect that has been studied a great deal over recent years: Multicultural London English.

## 3.5.2 Multicultural London English (MLE)

MLE is the term used by a group of linguists (primarily Jenny Cheshire, Paul Kerswill and Sue Fox) to describe the language they were hearing and recording in London between 2004 and 2010, especially in areas in which there was a wide variety of ethnicities and different heritage languages. Rather than see it as a separate variety of English, they view MLE as 'a repertoire of features', again emphasising the fluidity of speech.

The repertoire of features is selected by individuals from a 'feature pool' – a collection of words, grammar and pronunciations from all the different languages and dialects found in London. These features are available for anyone to use, so get taken up by individuals and groups of speakers to become part of their speech, often modified in the process. And while it might be possible to trace individual features back to their source languages, dialects or ethnolects, the process has in fact now made them ethnically neutral.

The process of selecting or acquiring features from the feature pool is one that is both conscious and unconscious. Unconsciously, it is quite predictable that children and young people will acquire the linguistic features that they are surrounded by. One outcome of the arrival of many different languages in an area is that there are fewer native speakers of the majority language (English) to serve as a model. The result is that children born in London begin to acquire English from their exposure to non-native varieties of English, which will obviously lead to a different variety of English than in previous generations. Crucially, this is the same for children of all ethnicities. In this scenario, the particular features an individual acquires has more to do with the frequency with which they are exposed to them rather than the colour of their skin or their ethnic background.

Consciously, young people may choose to use particular features that they see as attractive, or which seem to relate to their social practices or friendship networks. Often this has involved the adoption of features associated with 'Black' and Caribbean varieties of English. This is nothing new, as many young people throughout recent history have routinely gravitated towards Caribbean (and African American) youth culture, usually via music. The frequent adoption of such features is undoubtedly what is behind the depiction of MLE speakers of whatever ethnicity as 'sounding black' by outsiders. This perception is neatly summed up by the term often used in the mainstream media to describe MLE: Jafaican. The issue of 'sounding black' is one you will explore in more detail shortly.

Even though MLE shouldn't be thought of or described as a separate variety of English, there are specific features which make up the repertoire. Some of the main ones are as follows:

- Shorter trajectories for the vowel sounds in FACE, GOAT, MOUTH, PRICE. What this means is that while these vowel sounds involve considerable movement of the mouth in a traditional London accent, in MLE there is much less, if any, movement. In other words, the vowels have changed from being diphthongs to being monophthongs in some cases.

- The GOOSE vowel is pronounced differently. The vowel sound in words such as 'food', 'true' and 'crew' is pronounced further forward in the mouth, almost resembling the pronunciation of the French vowel in words like *tu*. This is actually a change that is occurring in all varieties of English, but it is a lot more extreme in MLE.

- Word-initial th-stopping: words beginning with 'th' are pronounced with /d/ or /t/, so 'they', 'the', 'there' become 'dey', 'dem', 'dere', and 'three', 'think', 'thing' become 'tree', 'tink', 'ting'.

- Use of the pragmatic marker 'You get me?' used in a similar way to how 'innit?' used to be used at the end of a sentence.

- Use of /ðə/ rather than /ði:/ for 'the'; and the use of 'a' /ə/ rather than 'an' /ən/, even before vowels. So instead of /ði:/ 'apple' and /ən/ 'apple', we get /ðə/ 'apple' and /ə/ 'apple'.

# 3.5.3 Multicultural Urban British English (MUBE)

Of course, London is not the only city in which young people are speaking differently from how they used to. As all large cities in the UK have some areas which are ethnically and linguistically diverse (as in London) it is likely that similar processes of language change are happening in those areas as well. However, this is not to say that everyone will be speaking in exactly the same way, as each city will already have its own regional accent features. Instead, there will be an underlying repertoire of shared features (an idea that Rob Drummond has named Multicultural Urban British English, or MUBE) with each city maintaining those accent features which are central to regional identity.

For example, while young people in Manchester are clearly using features associated with MLE in their speech, they haven't lost those features which mark them out as being from the north of England. They still pronounce the vowels FOOT/STRUT and TRAP/BATH in the same way for instance (see Chapter 1). At this stage it's too early to say for sure that there is a clearly identifiable MUBE, as more research needs to be carried out in the various UK cities. However, it seems very likely.

One very accessible way of investigating the existence of MUBE is by looking at grime music, as you did in Chapter 1. That chapter identified how the language of the original (London-based) grime artists was unmistakably MLE, yet as the music has spread from London, the accents have adapted. While grime artists from London still use MLE, there are noticeable local accent features in the performances of artists such as Bugzy Malone (Manchester), Lady Leshurr (Birmingham) and Astroid Boys (Cardiff). Grime is especially interesting in relation to ethnicity, as despite drawing on musical styles that have traditionally been associated with Black British culture, it can in many ways be seen as a racially inclusive genre. Grime is also a very likely mechanism for the spreading of linguistic features between cities, as it is a style of music that often involves active participation rather than passive listening.

Listen to grime artist Lady Leshurr's 'Queen's speech episode 4' (www.cambridge.org/links/escdiv6018). Notice how her GOAT vowel displays her regional (Birmingham area) accent in words such as 'over' and 'uploaded'. Her STRUT vowel is clearly not MLE, as she uses /ʊ/ in words such as 'club' and 'couple'. Also, the lettER vowel at the end of words like 'banter' is very typical of the region (it sounds more like 'banta'). But there are still lots of MLE/MUBE features alongside this, such as th-stopping in 'that' and 'thing', and a Jamaican-influenced pronunciation of 'gyal'.

Figure 3.4: Lady Leshurr clearly uses some local Birmingham features in her lyrics

Now listen to Bugzy Malone's track 'Spitfire' (www.cambridge.org/links/escdiv6019). Like Lady Leshurr, he has the northern British English STRUT vowel, with /ʊ/ in words such as 'Bugzy', under' and 'trust'. But unlike her, he has the very specific Manchester lettER vowel at the end of words like 'spitfire'. He also has a typically Manchester happY vowel in words such as 'money'. Again, there are still lots of MLE/MUBE features such as the th-stopping in 'this' and 'that', and the very fronted GOOSE vowel in words such as 'student' and 'two'.

Figure 3.5: Bugzy leaves no doubt as to his Manchester roots

Whatever the outcome of ongoing and future research, the existence of MLE and a possible MUBE tells us some very interesting things about language and ethnicity. You discovered earlier that MLE/MUBE can be seen as ethnically neutral in the sense that it is available to be used by anybody, whatever their race or ethnicity. This is despite the fact that 'outsiders' such as mainstream media or social commentators will often describe its use as people 'sounding black'. This is nothing new – people have been discussing white youth sounding black (and black youth sounding white) since at least the 1950s, both in the UK and the US. The discussion usually focuses on the conscious adoption of particular speech styles and features by individuals in order to align themselves with black youth culture. But something different is happening here.

The fact is that many young people no longer associate some of the features of MLE/MUBE with black varieties of English – they simply see them as part of 'teenage' English. While to outsiders (and possibly older outsiders especially) some of the features and speech styles they hear remind them of particular ethnolects, that same connection has become much less strong in the minds of the young people themselves, and in some cases has disappeared completely.

One of the young people in Rob Drummond's study (Drummond 2016) made the following point when he was asked if ethnicity mattered in relation to the way people speak:

Jordan      It does when you're using words like [Jamaican swear word]. I don't know what it means but that's different, I never used that word in my life. Because if I used that I'd know myself I'd sound like [an idiot].

| Researcher | Right. So who can use that and not sound like [an idiot]? |
|---|---|
| Jordan | Someone who matches the race or where tha- where it's from. |
| Researcher | I see. |
| Jordan | Cos you just sound stupid. But it's true. |
| Res | Yeah, so what if... |
| Jordan | *Rass* is fine. |

This is a very intelligent interpretation of language change in relation to ethnicity. It hints at the process whereby words, structures or sounds that are initially seen as unusual, marked, or belonging to a certain (ethnic) social group gradually become less unusual until they are accepted as unmarked features of a particular variety. To Jordan at least, the word 'rass' (a kind of exclamation, of Jamaican origin) is simply part of his everyday speech, but the swear word has not yet reached that status, and still 'belongs' to a particular ethnicity. (Incidentally, the fact that this is a swear word is probably not relevant here in terms of whether it could be used, it was a word commonly heard among other young people, and Jordan was not averse to the idea of swearing!) It seems that many of the features of MLE/MUBE are going through the same process. But what is interesting is that different people view them as being at different stages of that process, leading to very different feelings towards the use of such features.

## RESEARCH QUESTION
### The representation of (multi)ethnolects in the media

Look at the ways in which what linguists know as ethnolects and multiethnolects are represented in the media. How do these representations compare:

- with each other
- with what you have learned in this chapter/elsewhere in your studies
- with your own opinions?

Below are some links to relevant articles and blog posts to get you started.

- 'Forget Butty... it's Bruv now, innit! Behind the new 'Jafaican' dialect on the streets of Wales. Wales Online': www.cambridge.org/links/escdiv6020

- 'David Starkey claims "the whites have become black"', *The Guardian*/BBC *Newsnight* (video): www.cambridge.org/links/escdiv6021

- 'Why are so many middle-class children speaking in Jamaican patois? A father of an 11-year-old girl laments a baffling trend', Mail Online: www.cambridge.org/links/escdiv6022

- 'Ghetto grammar robs the young of a proper voice', *Evening Standard*: www.cambridge.org/links/escdiv6023

- 'Language is Power'. BBC Radio 4, *Four Thought:* www.cambridge.org/links/escdiv6024

- 'Multicultural London English is not "Jafaican"', Dialect Blog: www.cambridge.org/links/escdiv6025

- 'Thoughts on Lindsay Johns and "Ghetto Grammar"', Urben ID: www.cambridge.org/links/escdiv6026

- 'Dissing ghetto grammar to Mikey G and Funkmaster David C', EngLangBlog: www.cambridge.org/links/escdiv6027

- 'Jafaican it? No we're not', *The Guardian:* www.cambridge.org/links/escdiv6028

## ACTIVITY 3.3
### Who can use what?

Are you aware of any words, phrases or pronunciations that 'belong' to or are more associated with specific ethnic groups in your particular area/country? Do you think this is changing, as in the quoted transcript between Jordan and the researcher?

3

## 3.6 Whiteness

Accents and dialects (see Chapter 1) are often discussed in relation to a perceived standard. Although linguists see all varieties of language as equal, the very fact that there is the concept of a standard variety automatically makes one variety unmarked and normal, and another variety marked, or different. This situation is felt even more strongly in the area of language and ethnicity. Just as people who have an accent or dialect close to the standard (whatever that might be in their particular society) are often seen as 'not having an accent', people whose ethnicity is the same as that of the dominant norm in a society are seen as not having an ethnic identity. The result of this, in Europe and the US at least, is that 'whiteness', rather than being an ethnicity in itself, is actually viewed as the absence of ethnicity.

This perceived absence of ethnicity can lead to a huge social imbalance. It means that speakers of white varieties of English are seen as normal; they go unnoticed as part of the dominant system, controlling access to education and positions of power (see *Language and Power* in this series for a discussion of issues related to this). Speakers of 'ethnic' varieties of English on the other hand are different, and as such do not have the same automatic advantages.

The perception of ethnicity can be incredibly powerful. Donald Rubin (1992) carried out a fascinating experiment in which 62 native-English-speaking students listened to a recorded lecture. During the lecture, the students were shown a photograph of the 'lecturer'; however, half saw a picture of a European-American woman, and the other half saw a picture of an Asian woman. Incredibly, the students who saw the picture of the Asian woman rated the lecturer's accent as being 'more Asian', despite both groups having listened to precisely the same recording. The experiment is described in more detail in Lippi-Green (1997).

## 3.7 Crossing

Another illustration of the imbalance around language and ethnicity is the reaction to individuals using features of speech that do not 'belong' to their ethnicity. You have seen that views on what does or does not belong to a particular group of people are possibly changing, at least in the minds of young people. But still, at the moment, it will generally be noticed when people adopt particular speech features from a different ethnolect. What is particularly interesting is that when this process happens in the direction of a white-variety speaker adopting non-white features, it has a name – crossing. Yet when it happens in the other direction – with a non-white speaker using white features, there is no equivalent name. The underlying assumption appears to be that it is almost expected for people who speak non-standard non-white varieties to adopt the language of power, so it goes unnoticed. In his excellent chapter on ethnicity, sociolinguist Gerard Van Herk (2012) makes the point that such a change will of course not go unnoticed by people within the non-white community, who will certainly have names for this type of crossing.

## KEY TERM

**Crossing:** the practice of using particular features of speech that 'belong' to a different ethnicity from that of the speaker

In this chapter you have explored the very complex issue of ethnicity in relation to language. You have looked at some examples of speech features that are associated with particular ethnicities, and you have seen how such features can be used strategically within interaction in order to perform ethnic identities. In doing so, you understand how ethnicity, along with other aspects of our identities, is a fluid concept that cannot be fixed. MLE and MUBE were introduced as possible examples of a multiethnolect, in which linguistic features exist as a repertoire, available to be used by anybody, regardless of ethnicity. However, you have also seen how many language features are still widely perceived as 'belonging' to particular ethnic groups.

## PRACTICE QUESTION
### The role of ethnicity in the use of language

Evaluate the idea that a person's ethnicity will always play an important part in their language use.

# Wider reading

You can find out more about the topics in this chapter by reading the following:

Kaplan, A. (2016) *Women Talk More than Men... And Other Myths about Language Explained.* Cambridge: Cambridge University Press. Chapter 2 looks at African American English as part of the discussion around dialect.

Mooney, A. and Evans, B. (2015) *Language, Society & Power: An Introduction* (Fourth edition). Oxon: Routledge. Chapter 7 deals with ethnicity.

Van Herk, G. (2012) *What is Sociolinguistics?* Malden: Wiley-Blackwell. Chapter 6 deals with ethnicity.

# Chapter 4
# Global diversity

In this chapter you will:

- Look at the ways in which different groups of people around the world use English

- Study some examples of different World Englishes

- Evaluate the debates and arguments that take place about the place of English in the world

# 4.1 English around the world

In the chapters so far, you have looked largely at English language diversity in the UK. In this chapter, you will start to consider the ways in which English is used around the rest of the world, its uses and functions and how it has come to be seen as a global language. This is a huge, and rapidly expanding, topic, so what follows is only the beginning of what you could study. Suggestions are given throughout the chapter for further research and study, and wider reading is recommended at the end.

The growth of English around the world has been a long process. In the early 1600s, English only had 5–7 million speakers (the vast majority of whom were in England itself) and now has somewhere between 1.5 and 2 billion speakers (most of them outside the UK, whose population is only around 60 million): this is a huge increase and there is no sign of it slowing down.

This growth has been a contentious process, sometimes associated with colonisation, violent repression and ruthless political policy, but could also be viewed as a natural expansion, linked to the movement of people around the globe and the need for a shared means of communication that many people can understand and make use of. These different perspectives will be considered later in the chapter along with debates about the nature of the English used around the world and its relationship to English in the UK.

Figure 4.1: It's English, but not as we know it

> ### ACTIVITY 4.1
> #### 'I have bumblebees in the bottom'
> Look at Figure 4.1, which shows examples of English written by non-native English language users. What do you notice about the ways in which English is used and how it varies from what you might expect to see in Standard British English?

## 4.1.1 Where English began

English began life as Anglo-Saxon, reflecting some of its roots in the languages of the Angles and the Saxons, both Northern European tribes who settled in the British Isles during this period. English first appeared in the fifth century CE and took centuries to become firmly established as the main language in its own country, let alone spread to other countries. This might seem like a strange idea from a modern perspective, but English as a language was generally looked down upon in the UK until the fifteenth century when it became more firmly established as the language of the ruling elite and thus acquired the status it needed to become a national language. Indeed, the notion of the country of 'England' as it is now known was not really established until the rule of King Alfred in the ninth century CE and it was much later still that English came to be seen as the language of the nation state.

While English was widely spoken, the languages that were preferred by the Church and the state were Latin and – after the Norman Invasion of 1066 – Norman French. English was the spoken language of the main population but it was not seen as a language fit for the high offices of state.

The *Cambridge Topics in English Language* title, *Language Change* offers more detailed discussion of the growth of English as a language and the debates about its uses and functions, but in summary English grew in status through the fourteenth to seventeenth centuries. During this time, English came to be used in teaching, law, religion, government and science. By the eighteenth century, it was well enough established for educated people to argue about its correct use and to publish numerous books about grammar, spelling and 'proper' speech.

> ### ACTIVITY 4.2
> #### Before English
> English was not the first language spoken in the British Isles. Try to find out as much as you can about the ways in which the languages of the world have developed by looking at the following websites and blogs.

Which languages were spoken in the UK before English and where did they come from?

- www.cambridge.org/links/escdiv6029

- www.cambridge.org/links/escdiv6030

- www.cambridge.org/links/escdiv6031

In some respects, the development of English as a national language sowed the seeds for its growth as an international language. While the 'grammarians' of the eighteenth century argued about the details of language, they were also busy defining the parameters of a language that could represent and celebrate the developing nation state. In a way, by defining what English as language was like, they were also defining what England as a nation might be. And by this time, English (the language) was already starting to move away from England (the country) and into other countries, beginning its steady spread around the globe and its growth as a world language and a language made up of elements from other parts of the world. Philip Seargeant (2012) notes:

> Thus, while within Britain a standard language ideology was developing which was regularizing aspects of the language, as English was being spread abroad it necessarily became mixed and diversified. This happened both in terms of the different British dialects that were being exported – the colonial process brought together people from different areas of Britain, and, to an extent, different social classes – and in the ways the language was adapted to the contexts in which it was being used. (Seargeant 2012)

For example, the different types of English that went into the formation of varieties such as Australian and New Zealand English – elements of London English, Irish and Scots English, along with that spoken in many other larger cities – played a part in shaping what these varieties would become in the future. And it was not just the English growing in new territories that diversified: as English reached new places, it brought back with it – and integrated into its own vocabulary – new words. The Early Modern English period (1450–1700) saw a rapid growth in the English lexicon, some of which was influenced by words that were imported from the Americas, Africa and India.

## ACTIVITY 4.3
### Word origins

Look up the etymologies (word origins) of the following words in the English vocabulary. Which languages and which parts of the world have they come from? What might this tell you about the global reach of English?

- Pyjamas
- Bungalow
- Assassin
- Thug

- Mohawk
- Tattoo
- Kosher

# 4.2 Where English has gone

English is used all around the world now and has a home in every continent, but it reached various locations at different times. While in this instantly connected age of telecommunications, language can spread around the world in a moment, in the past, English moved at the speed of the fastest form of transport, whether that was on foot, on horseback, or on board a ship (Figure 4.2). English first moved from England to other parts of the British Isles – Scotland, Wales and Ireland – before making the journey across the Atlantic to the Americas and then to Africa, India, Australia and dozens of other territories.

Figure 4.2: The spread of English

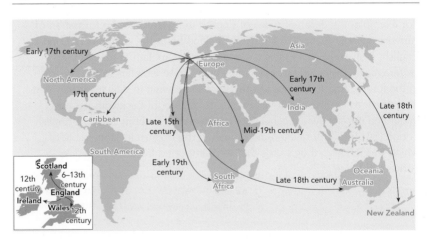

# 4.2.1 The British Isles

Some of the first staging posts on the journey of English beyond its own borders were other parts of the British Isles. In Scotland, Wales and Ireland, Standard English was established alongside, and often in opposition to, local forms. Scottish Standard English grew in the seventeenth and eighteenth centuries, in a country where Scots, 'the direct descendant of the Northumbrian form of Old English planted in south-eastern Scotland between 525 and 633' (Johnston 2007) was already established.

In Wales, English made inroads from the eighth century onwards but it was not until the twelfth century, as Robert Penhallurick (2007) explains, that English 'incursions into Welsh territory (were) significant enough to mark the beginnings of the long process of Anglicisation. These incursions came in the wake of the Normans, who established strongholds through the north and south of Wales'. As Penhallurick goes on to say, 'from the end of the nineteenth century, English can be considered the majority language in Wales' (Penhallurick 2007).

Ireland was a more complicated picture. Raymond Hickey (2007) explains that, 'The English language was taken to Ireland with the settlers from Britain who arrived in the late twelfth century. Since then the fate of the English has been closely linked with that of the Irish language which it came largely to replace in the late modern period' (Hickey 2007). The movement of people from Scotland to the north of Ireland brought in Scots English while in the south of Ireland, a separate form developed.

In all three countries, Celtic languages also existed and, with the advance of English, these were pushed to the fringes. For example, during the period 1200–1600, Irish was the dominant language in Ireland but by the eighteenth century English was widespread and by the time of the Great Famine (1846–48) Padraig O'Riagain states that only '30% of the population were Irish speaking, mostly in Western regions' (2007). The famine led to over a million lives being lost and many of these were Irish speakers. The movement of rural people to larger towns, because of the famine, further fragmented the place of Irish and the introduction of the national school system in 1830, in which the teaching of English was preferred and the use of Irish actively discouraged, made this more acute.

Welsh, Scots and Irish are all still spoken in their respective countries and have undergone something of a revival in the late twentieth and early twenty-first centuries, but English is the dominant language in all three countries. However, this is not necessarily viewed as a positive situation by all speakers of the indigenous languages. The forms of English used in these countries vary in a number of ways from Standard English as well and more details about these variations can be found in the Wider Reading section and texts mentioned above.

> ### ACTIVITY 4.4
> #### English around the British Isles
> Use the MacMillan Dictionary Blog website (www.cambridge.org/
> links/escdiv6032) to research and investigate the main ways in which
> Scottish, Welsh and Irish English differ from each other and from
> Standard English, in terms of phonology, lexis and grammar.

## 4.2.2 The USA

English first appeared in what is now the USA in the late sixteenth and early
seventeenth centuries, with the first permanent settlement established in
Jamestown Virginia in 1607. Other settlements followed and many of these
were made up of people who were seeking religious freedom and to escape
persecution: forerunners of the modern word 'refugee', it could be argued.

These immigrants brought with them a range of language varieties. As linguist
David Crystal explains:

> The two settlements – one in Virginia, to the south, the other to the north,
> in present-day New England – had different linguistic backgrounds. Although
> the southern colony brought settlers from several parts of England, many
> of them came from England's 'West Country' – such counties as Somerset
> and Gloucestershire – and brought with them its characteristic accent with
> its 'Zummerzet' voicing of 's' sounds, and the 'r' strongly pronounced after
> vowels (…) By contrast, many of the Plymouth colonists came from the east
> of England – in particular, Lincolnshire, Nottinghamshire, Essex, Kent and
> London, with some from the Midlands and further afield. These eastern
> accents were rather different – notable lacking an 'r' after vowels – and they
> proved to be the dominant influence in this area. (Crystal 2003)

The indigenous people – the Native Americans – appear to have had little
influence on the new American English that was starting to form, beyond a few
lexical items (words such as 'skunk', 'cougar', 'tomahawk' and 'squash') which
themselves were often approximations of the original words used. Dick Leith
argues that this is because 'the language of a conquered people has little effect
on that of the conquerors' (Leith 2007).

Much of the rest of the early history of American English is a history of immigration,
from Ireland, Scotland, Spain, the Netherlands and Germany, among others.
But also, and tellingly for later developments in the language and culture of the
USA, the slave trade brought many thousands of Africans. As Crystal outlines:
'A population of little more than 2,500 black slaves in 1700 had become about
100,000 by 1775, far out-numbering the southern whites' (Crystal 2003).

While new arrivals brought with them different native languages, many of these were quickly swallowed up into the wider pool of American English or jettisoned for the language that was already taking root. American vocabulary, as the seminal American writer H.L. Mencken notes, 'tends to grow richer and freer every year' (Mencken 1919) and makes use of a range of 'materials' to create new language. New words come about through contact with other languages but other words take existing lexis from British English and shape it in different forms. Mencken refers to 'boot' and 'shoe' as taking different paths in UK and US English, along with 'shop' and 'store'. Some American words have meanings or grammatical forms that once existed in UK English but which have changed in one place but not the other. So, British 'Autumn' and US 'Fall' describe the same season of the year, but the latter was once used frequently in the UK. 'Gotten' as a participle form of the verb 'to get' is seen as non-standard (or just plain wrong) in British English and standard in American, but again was once common in the UK and remains in older expressions such as 'woe-begotten' and 'ill-gotten gains' or the more familiar 'forgotten'.

## ACTIVITY 4.5

### Separated by a common language

Research the words in the table below and see if you can find the US or UK equivalent required in each space. Explore the etymology of each of these terms, using a source such as the *Oxford English Dictionary* online or the Merriam-Webster Dictionary. Where are they from? In which country did they first appear?

| UK | USA |
| --- | --- |
|  | Apartment |
|  | Sidewalk |
| Tramp |  |
|  | Elevator |
| Trousers |  |

# 4.2.3 Other places

The movement of English around the world is often described by linguists as taking the form of two distinct diasporas, the nature of which often influences the shape of the English being used in those countries subsequently.

## KEY TERM

**Diaspora:** a dispersal or spreading out from a central point

According to World Englishes expert Jennifer Jenkins, these diasporas are characterised in the following ways:

> The first diaspora involved relatively large-scale migrations of mother-tongue English speakers from England, Scotland and Ireland predominantly to North America, Australia and New Zealand. (Jenkins 2015)

In these countries, English became established as mother tongue varieties, spoken by large numbers of people and gradually changing to meet the needs of the users.

> The second diaspora took place at various points during the eighteenth and nineteenth centuries in very different ways and with very different results from those of the first diaspora. (Jenkins 2015)

---

**KEY TERM**

**Mother tongue variety:** the language that a person learns first as a child

---

In the countries of the second diaspora – Nigeria, Kenya, India and Singapore, for example – colonisation led to the establishment of second-language varieties, or what Jenkins refers to as 'New Englishes'. You can read more about the ways in which English reached many of these countries in the *Cambridge Topics in English Language* book, *Language Change*, or in the suggested wider reading at the end of this chapter, but in the next section you will look at examples of how English varies in some of these areas.

# 4.3 How English varies around the world

Along with the specific varieties of English around the world that you have looked at so far, there are some wider patterns that can be discerned when looking at World Englishes. Some of these patterns are related to the functions of English – what it is used for – and the contexts in which it is used, but there are also linguistic characteristics that are common to many of the different Englishes. It is probably worth remembering that any language will vary, depending on the uses to which it is put. Indeed, English in the UK varies along a continuum from the most formal written variety to the most conversational spoken form and this will also be affected by factors such as:

- how well you know someone

- the expectations of the different participants

- the setting and immediate context

- the mode through which you communicate.

English around the world is no different. A language user might use a very colloquial style that mixes elements of English with another language when talking to a friend or swapping online messages with a family member, but might switch to a much more formal kind of English in a work setting.

## 4.3.1 Phonology

One of the most noticeable forms of variation between World Englishes is the way in which different sounds are realised. Consonants and vowels vary in their pronunciation from place to place, but also the stress patterns placed on syllables within words differ. You can see a lot more about phonological variation in Chapter 1 but some noticeable examples of global variation are included here.

- Words like 'cot' and 'caught' would be pronounced differently in most forms of UK English, but would sound the same in many varieties of North American English. Have a look at the lexical set of CLOTH/NORTH in Chapter 1 (Table 1.2) to see this alongside other vowel differences.

- Words like 'sit' and 'seat' would sound very similar when spoken in Nigerian or Ghanaian English.

- Consonants such as /r/ and /w/ pose problems for different speakers for whom these are not familiar sounds, so for example an Indian English speaker might replace /w/ with /v/ in a word like 'water'.

- The 'th' sound in words like 'that' and 'thought' is pronounced differently (as /ð/ and /θ/). These are often changed to /f/ and /v/ respectively.

- Rhoticity, a feature mentioned in Chapter 1, relates to the pronunciation of the /r/ in words like 'park' and 'farm'. It varies around the UK but has very different social connotations in the USA, with rhotic speakers often being viewed as of a higher status, whereas in the UK rhoticity is often seen as a marker of a rural, working class identity and therefore less prestigious.

- English uses a stress-based intonation, where the stress on certain syllables follows a regular pattern (often unstressed followed by stressed). Syllable-based languages such as Yoruba, French and Hindi have a pattern in which all syllables follow a regular pattern, whether stressed or not, and this often transfers into how English is spoken.

## 4.3.2 Vocabulary

Words vary from place to place within the UK but on a global level this variation is even more noticeable. When English has reached different countries, it has often made use of local words to expand its own lexicon. In the places where those languages are still used, a more varied and rich vocabulary often exists, incorporating and blending many local words alongside English words.

In South Asia, for example, you can find words such as *dosa* and *roti* borrowed from Indian languages being used around the world to describe types of bread, but also hybrid (or compounded) forms of words such as *congresswallah* which combines an English word with a Hindi word or suffix for 'person' or 'someone who does a job'.

In South-East Asia, there are many borrowings from the Malay language and what Nicola Galloway and Heath Rose (2015) refer to as 'semantic extensions': words which have taken on a wider meaning in a different location. For example, Singapore English uses the verb 'open' to also mean 'turn on' as in 'open the light'.

## 4.3.3 Grammar

Word order and morphology vary across different varieties of English around the world and some of the key patterns are noted later in section 4.4 on English as a *Lingua Franca* (ELF). A common pattern is for plural endings on count nouns to either be unmarked or marked using a different system. For example, 'I have many book' does not mark the plural on the noun 'book' and 'the gyal dem' (the girls) marks it using 'dem', while what would normally be seen as non-count nouns often become plurals. So, nouns like 'information' or 'furniture' would be pluralised to become 'informations' or 'furnitures'.

Tenses differ in their formation with usages such as 'I walk here yesterday' and 'I have been here ten years ago' showing that past action is conveyed in a range of ways.

Crystal (2003) identifies a large range of grammatical variation from the research literature – including 'I finish eat', 'I already eat' and 'Did you find?' – and you can find many more examples by following up some of the wider reading outlined at the end of this chapter.

### KEY TERMS

**Count noun:** a noun which refers to separate items that can be counted

**Non-count noun:** a noun which refers to something that cannot be counted or separated

## 4.3.4 Pragmatics

Beyond the literal meanings of words and phrases, is another layer of meaning that comes through implication and understanding of figures of speech. These are often phrases or sayings that have been passed down through the history of a language or rely on idiom. Clearly, these can pose problems because their literal meaning is not apparent. Why, for instance, should 'It's raining cats and dogs' mean 'It's raining heavily'?

On another level, communication relies on more than just words; cultural expectations around conventions such as turn-taking, politeness and even how loudly people should speak can vary.

## KEY TERM

**Idiom:** an expression or phrase that is commonly used but whose meaning is not literal (e.g. 'to kick the bucket' means 'to die'). Such expressions often have ancient historical origins

## ACTIVITY 4.6

### Using the corpus

Text 4A and Text 4B consist of answers to exam questions written by learners of English from around the world. What kinds of patterns can you identify in the way in which each student uses English in their answer?

### Text 4A

It is said that, when you meet someone for the first time, the first impression you get from him, is the one that usually makes you like or dislike him and generally is very important in shaping the opinion about the person you've just met. However, sometimes, this very first impression, can make you reach wrong conclusion, and therefore it can effect your attitude in a way that later, you may regret for it.

I'm afraid that the latter happened to me in the case of my friendship with Alex. We have been close friends for more than a decade now, sharing our secrets, every pleasant and unpleasant moment of our life. This so strong relationship that has been developed between us two make me now feel emparassment whenever I recall the first time I met him.

From the Cambridge Learner Corpus

Text 4B

Dear Jack,

Thank you for your letter to me. How are you? I apologize for not writing you since about two months now. This is because I was very busy. What you wrote in your letter about the situation here (in my country) is of course exaggerated. It is true that, there was a strike for about two months. But now the strike has ended. And people are trying one way or the other to adopt to the new situation.

The people went on strike because life is going bad and bad every day. An Engineer cannot avoid going to his work by car everyday, because petrol is too expensive you can imagine that. The situation here is too difficult. There is no electricity from ten (a.m) to six (p.m) everyday. Our Government said that there were no coal. You see we are living like the third world people here but now after the strike. Things are coming back to normal. Now we have free medical care. Before the strike we pay for medical care. A week in the hospital cost more than an Engineering salary for the whole month.

From the Cambridge Learner Corpus

## RESEARCH QUESTION
### World Englishes

Pick one or more of the following varieties of World Englishes and use the websites suggested in Activity 4.2 (and the wider reading at the end of this chapter) to put together a range of examples about how the variety differs in key linguistic areas from Standard English in the UK (and your own variety of English). Find out as much as you can about the history of the variety – when it arrived, how it has been used and attitudes towards its use – and then consider how you could use this information in the practice question that follows.

- Malaysian English

- Caribbean English

- South African English

- Australian English

- New Zealand English

- Nigerian English

- Indian English

- Singapore English

# 4.4 English as a *lingua franca* (ELF)

One of the more recent developments in thinking about World Englishes is to see English as a *lingua franca*. A lingua franca is a language used between speakers who have no common language between them, to enable communication for purposes such as trade. *Lingua francas* are built on a base language, which tends to be a global language such as English, for obvious reasons. Thus, English is the world's most common *lingua franca*, and Swahili, Arabic, French, Spanish, Hindi, Portuguese and several others are also used in this way, to a much lesser extent. English is not the world's first – or only – *lingua franca* (Latin and Persian have served those roles in the past, to varying degrees) but it is definitely the most widely used.

**KEY TERM**

**Lingua franca:** a language used to communicate between people who speak different languages

A *lingua franca* is often described as an 'auxiliary' language, used for functional rather than social purposes, and speakers are just as likely to be native users as they are non-native. It is a convenient method of communication to serve global human relations, and is appreciated by millions worldwide. Crucially, when English is used as a *lingua franca* (ELF), it is not a variety as such, with specific features, but something that changes to suit the needs of its users at a given time and in a given context. Jennifer Jenkins (2006) lists five common characteristics of English as a *lingua franca*:

1   It provides a mutually intelligible language, used by speakers of different languages allowing them to communicate with one another.

2   It is an alternative to English as a Foreign Language, rather than a replacement – it serves a functional communicative purpose rather than being associated with education.

3   It is just as likely to include elements of Standard English as well as linguistic features reflective of more local forms.

4    Accommodation and code-switching are common practice during *lingua franca* communication.

5    Language proficiency in speakers may be low or high.

In terms of the linguistic structure of English as a *lingua franca*, Barbara Seidlhofer (2004) identifies the following typical characteristics:

- non-use of the third-person present tense *–s* ('she look very sad')

- interchangeable use of the relative pronouns *who* and *which* ('a book who'; 'a person which')

- omission of the definite and indefinite articles where they are obligatory in native speaker English and insertion where they do not occur in native speaker English

- use of an all-purpose question tag such as 'isn't it?' or 'no?' instead of 'shouldn't they?' ('they should arrive soon, isn't it?')

- increasing of redundancy by adding prepositions ('we have to study about') or by increasing explicitness ('blue colour' vs. 'blue' and 'how long time?' vs. 'how long?')

- heavy reliance on certain verbs of high semantic generality, such as 'do', 'have', 'make', 'put' and 'take'

- pluralisation of nouns which are considered uncountable in native speaker English ('informations', 'staffs', 'advices')

- use of *that*-clauses instead of infinitive constructions ('I want that we discuss about my dissertation').

These characteristics demonstrate that English is shaped as much by its non-native speakers as by its native speakers and that is hardly surprising given the sheer weight of numbers involved: many hundreds of millions of people using English are not doing so as native users. However, there is still some dispute among linguists about the exact relationship between different varieties of World Englishes and ELF. One significant question to be asked is whether a single form of English might develop as a *lingua franca* – perhaps becoming a kind of global standard – or, as ELF clearly proposes, if a more fluid and flexible use of language that varies according to its users and immediate needs will spring up wherever there is a need.

Many people adopt the rather prescriptive view that *lingua francas* are somehow inferior or deficient forms of a language, with crude and basic grammatical and phonological systems. Jennifer Jenkins (2015) discusses the implications of this – that there can be a bias against non-native forms such as *lingua francas*, because of a preference for the 'correct' native forms of English. She argues that speakers should have a choice about the forms they use, and that the use of standard, native forms is unnecessary for most of the world's English speakers.

Indeed, the whole link between England (the country) and English (the language) has been critiqued by the linguist Mario Saraceni (2011) who argues that existing models for explaining the relationship between World Englishes foreground what he calls 'the metaphor of "spread"' which creates a fundamental problem.

> If the presence of English in the world is seen as based on a centre-periphery relationship, the periphery will be characterised by Englishes which have been modified and adapted to suit local environments, while the centre, by contrast, will be strongly connected with an unadulterated form of English, reinforcing the belief in a sort of linguistic garden of Eden, where English is pure and perfect, or, at least, authentic. This perpetuates the much-exploited possibility that Englishes can be placed along an equally arbitrary scale of 'quality', 'authenticity', 'purity', 'correctness' and so on. Altered forms of English, meanwhile, will perhaps arouse interest and curiosity, but are unlikely to gain the sort of recognition that is aspired to primarily among World Englishes scholars. (Saraceni 2011)

Saraceni's argument is that rather than view English as belonging to any one group more than another, or one variety of English to be seen as more 'genuine' than another, a different focus should be explored. The communicative uses to which people put English in their own individual way – as part of a linguistic repertoire, probably consisting of many other languages – should be at the heart of the discussion. As he explains:

> … strategies of negotiation are far more important for mutual intelligibility than using identical linguistic forms and that linguistic closeness is attained through accommodation rather than exclusively via the possession of one shared code. (Saraceni 2011)

Naturally, this approach has been attacked by prescriptivists for its apparent absence of reference to a 'standard' form of English and its supposed *laissez-faire* perception that communication can be left to the individual needs of the speakers. Much like the debates about language variation and diversity in the UK, the arguments often come back to conflicting views on the role of a standard form and how closely it should be followed. Is there such a thing as a 'Global Standard English' that can be referred to by all English speakers wherever they are in the world and whatever they are doing? And if not, should there be one? This very question was at the heart of a debate between two eminent linguists in this field, Randolph Quirk and Braj Kachru.

Debating the issue between 1985 and 1990, often in the pages of the journal *English Today*, the two linguists adopted positions often characterised by their opponents as 'liberation linguistics' (on the part of Kachru) and 'deficit linguistics' (on the part of Quirk). For Quirk, it is important to adhere to a standard form of

English, with British English most likely to inform that standard. For Kachru, the argument is not over the need for standards but how and why certain standards should exist and who has control over them. He sees the reality of English language use as much more complicated to control and codify than Quirk and argues that in attempting to impose a central standard, not enough attention has been paid to the identity of the different Englishes found around the world.

# 4.5 Arguments about English

As you have already seen, the development of English around the world has been contentious. As English grows, other local languages can be forced out of use and even die out entirely. What is also interesting is to see how UK English is affected by the growth of other varieties of English around the world. In this section, you will look at the ways in which a particular variety of English – American English – has returned to the UK and influenced the home-grown variety.

## 4.5.1 American and UK English

It is not uncommon to hear complaints about American English such as the one below.

> Like the grey squirrels that were introduced into the UK from the U.S. 130 years ago — and have almost wiped out our indigenous (and much lovelier) red squirrels — American words are infectious, destructive and virulent. And they are taking over. (Stevens, 'Don't talk garbage… or why American words are mangling our English', *Daily Mail*, 30 May 2012)

For over a century American English has been perceived by some as a threat to British English. The growth of the USA as a world power throughout the twentieth century, not just in terms of its economy and international political role but its cultural and social influence, has led to an increased use of American English around the world. In fact, it might be argued that American English is a much more powerful and influential variety than UK English. Crystal explains it in this way:

> So much of the power which has fuelled the growth of the English language during the twentieth century has stemmed from America… the country contains nearly four times as many mother-tongue speakers of English as any other nation. It has been more involved with international developments in twentieth-century technology than any other nation. It is in control of the new industrial (that is, electronic) revolution. And it exercises a greater influence on the way English is developing worldwide

than does any other regional variety – often, of course, to the discomfiture of people in the UK, Australia, New Zealand, Canada and South Africa, who regularly express worries in their national presses about the onslaught of 'Americanisms'. (Crystal 2003)

These worries are often expressed using metaphors of invasion and plague: discourses that present American English as a threatening and dangerous outside influence. But it is not just the linguistic threat that exercises some British commentators. Writing for British right-wing newspaper *The Daily Mail* in 2010, the journalist Matthew Engel argued:

> Nowadays, people have no idea where American ends and English begins. And that's a disaster for our national self-esteem. We are in danger of subordinating our language to someone else's – and with it large aspects of British life. ('Say no to the get-go! Americanisms swamping English, so wake up and smell the coffee', Engel 2010)

Once again, arguments about language are used as a proxy for wider social and cultural concerns, in this case the global dominance and supposed cultural imperialism of the USA. So, to what extent are Stevens and Engel (and many others) correct that English has been influenced (or indeed taken over, invaded or infected) by American English? Certainly, there has been some movement from one side of the Atlantic to the other. In the early twentieth century, with the growth of the film industry, the word 'movies' first appeared in US English (first cited in the OED as 1909 for 'movies' and 1910 for 'movie') and then crossed the Atlantic to grow in popularity in the UK. Google n-grams can be used to chart the relative popularity of the terms (see Figures 4.3 and 4.4) and it can be seen how the use in the UK followed, but was less widespread than, US usage.

Figure 4.3: Google n-gram showing the frequency of the use of the word 'movie' in the USA over time

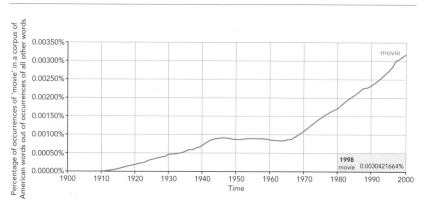

4

Figure 4.4: Google n-gram showing the usage frequency of the word 'movie' in the UK over time. (Note the different scale of the y-axis.)

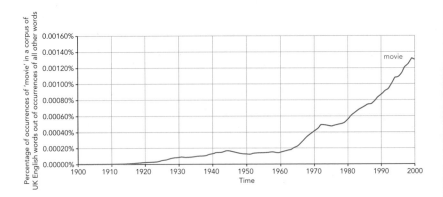

Writing in 1995, Henry Porter argued against doom-laden predictions about American English taking over and pointed out that the 'freshness and energy' of US English attracts many people to its use.

> So nearly 60 years ago they were worrying about the effect of imported slang, yet there is absolutely no sign that English English has been subsumed. The fact is that we take from America what we need or what amuses us. American English provides all sorts of vernaculars and jargons which we have not had the wit to invent. There is the criminal argot (mugging, hijack, rub out, stretch, bump off, third degree, junkie, hit man and whack), the showbiz talk (casting couch, deadpan, slapstick, one-night stand, bit part, showstopper, brat pack), and language from the psychiatrist's chair (psychobabble, schizoid, paranoid, psycho, shrink, stressed out).

> It is not just a matter of wit. America tends to develop things first and therefore the vocabulary which goes with these new inventions. It has been exposed to a range of immigrant influences which add to English and distort it with an admirable lack of propriety. The Jews who went from Europe to the States in the last century didn't give a fig for Johnson's Dictionary and the English spoken by Queen Victoria. Thus the US gained, as eventually did we, 'schmooz', 'schlepp', 'spiel', 'schnozzle', 'kosher' and constructions such as 'I should know already'. (Porter 1995)

American English (as a newer form of English) and America (as a newer and seemingly more dynamic and exciting nation) seem to carry positive associations which some people feel are more in tune with how they want to present themselves. Why – the argument goes – should I use a stuffy English word that has been around for centuries, when I can use a new and freshly minted American one?

Others argue that the impact of US English on UK English is overstated and frequently misunderstood. Lynne Murphy, an American linguist living and working in the UK, runs a blog called 'Separated by a Common Language' which features a range of discussion about American and English usage. Many of Murphy's articles correct misapprehensions about American English and its supposed ubiquity in UK English, with some providing fascinating case studies about how research can be used to counter myths about language.

## ACTIVITY 4.7
### Myths of American English

Use Murphy's blog (www.cambridge.org/links/escdiv6033) to identify a range of language issues associated with American and English usage. Select two or three examples of words and phrases that have been discussed and follow the discussions about these words. What do these tell you about some of the myths and panics over the supposed invasion of Americanisms?

Data gathered by Oxford University as part of the annual '500 Words' writing competition for children in the UK would suggest that young people are influenced to some extent by American vocabulary but also by language associated with events in the news, technology and popular culture. For example, in the 2016 competition, words such as those in Table 4.1 grew in popularity.

Table 4.1: Data from Oxford Children's Corpus Summary Report, 2016

|  | 2016 frequency | 2015 frequency |
|---|---|---|
| velociraptor/s (from films) | 368 | 93 |
| raptor/s (from films) | 360 | 69 |
| refugee/s (from contemporary events) | 339 | 67 |
| lightsaber/s (from films) | 267 | 48 |
| emoji/s (from popular culture) | 199 | 25 |
| spacewalk (from contemporary events) | 167 | 10 |
| stormtrooper/s (from films) | 123 | 19 |
| selkie/s (from folklore) | 119 | 19 |
| illuminati (from popular culture) | 108 | 14 |
| chipmunks (from films) | 101 | 21 |

In a separate project carried out by Lancaster University, to compile a new British National Corpus of spoken English (the *BNC2014*), out of 2 million words collected in 2014 and compared to the data from the original corpus collected in the early 1990s, the word 'awesome' has gained in popularity while 'marvellous' has diminished. Likewise, 'fortnight' has diminished in use and 'two weeks' increased. Is this conclusive proof of the Americanisation of English? Hardly. The completed *BNC2014* will prove a useful way of exploring trends in the vocabulary of British English though and perhaps shed some light on the influence of certain terms from the USA. Vocabulary is a fast-changing element of language and can provide a useful snapshot of language diversity and change, but it is not the only aspect of language worth exploring.

## 4.5.2 The problem with English

One further area of discussion to finish this chapter is that of the problems that UK English speakers have (or create) in their interactions with other English users around the world. Just as many people will claim not to have an accent, yet be able to identify everyone else as speaking with one, UK English speakers have their own varieties of English that they are unaware of and these are often quite different from the Standard English that many non-native speakers have learned.

Many forms of English make use of idiom and slang that are not instantly intelligible to outsiders, as this extract from an article by Spencer Hazel illustrates:

> Speakers who have English as their mother tongue can find themselves in a baffling predicament. While at home they are persuaded that the rest of the world now speaks their lingo. Abroad they discover that their own English renders them incomprehensible to colleagues and business partners. In one piece of research into English as the world's corporate language, a British expat in Scandinavia recounted: "When I started [in Denmark] I spoke I guess as I normally had done and wrote as I normally had done and people weren't getting me, they weren't understanding."

> Indeed, while her Danish colleagues were increasingly used to working in English with others from the wider international community, it was the native varieties that caused problems. Used to working with English speakers from all over Europe, a Spanish student in Denmark remarked to another researcher: "Now it's more difficult for me to understand the real English."

> What is more, this "real English"—which dizzyingly encompasses the whole range of dialects from Liverpool in England, to Wellington in New Zealand, via Johannesburg in South Africa, and Memphis in the US—is only the start of the problem.

### Communication breakdowns

When an American manager in Japan cannot understand why his Japanese staff will not give him the "ballpark figure" he has demanded, this breakdown in communication can lead to a real disintegration in workplace relations. And the underlying feelings of mistrust are mutual. The inability of the traveling native English speaker to refrain from homeland idiosyncrasies, subtextual dexterity, and cultural in-jokes has been found to result in resentment and suspicion.

International colleagues resent the lack of effort made on the part of the monoglot English speaker. They experience a loss of professional stature when having to speak with those who are not only comfortable with the language, but who appear to vaunt the effortlessness with which they bend the language to their will. And they suspect that the offending expat uses this virtuosity to gain unfair advantage in the workplace.

On a recent trip to Japan, a manager in an international consortium recounted to me how he and other international partners would hold back from actively contributing to meetings where his British and American partners dominated the floor. Following the meeting they would seek one another out to discuss matters between themselves in private.

This points to a very real danger that native English speakers, especially those who never mastered another language, risk missing out on business opportunities—whether in the form of contracts, idea development, job opportunities, and the like—due to a basic lack of understanding of what international English communication entails. (Hazel 2016)

## ACTIVITY 4.8
### Idioms or idiocy?

Re-read the section about communications breakdowns. Why are idiomatic or business English expressions problematic in international interactions?

The author goes on to suggest that 'This should be a wake-up call for politicians (...) Rather than laying the problems of English at the door of those who speak it as a second, third, or fourth language, it would be wise for mother-tongue nations to do more to prepare their professional classes for the language challenges they face abroad'. How far do you agree with this view?

# Wider reading

You can find out more about the topics in this chapter by reading the following:

## For comprehensive and detailed overviews of the growth of English around the world and connected debates

Crystal, D. (2003) *English as a Global Language* (Second edition). Cambridge: Cambridge University Press.

Galloway, N. and Rose, H. (2015) *Introducing Global Englishes*. London: Routledge.

Jenkins, J. (2015) *Global Englishes: A Resource Book for Students* (Third edition). London: Routledge.

Sergeant, P. (2012) *Exploring World Englishes: Language in a Global Context*. London: Routledge.

Setter, J. (2012) 'Englishes around the world'. In *Language: A Student Handbook of Key Topics and Theories* (ed. D. Clayton). London: EMC.

## For the debates between Quirk and Kachru referred to in this chapter

Seidlhofer, B. (2003) 'The Global Spread of English'. In *Controversies in Applied Linguistics*. Oxford: Oxford University Press.

## For more details about World Englishes, including models to explain their spread and growth

Rana, R. and Cushing, I. (2018) *Language Change* (*Cambridge Topics in English Language series*). Cambridge: Cambridge University Press.

Several websites offer good material on World Englishes, including these:

http://blog.oxforddictionaries.com/category/varieties-of-english/

www.bl.uk/learning/langlit/sounds/case-studies/minority-ethnic/

www.thehistoryofenglish.com/issues_global.html

# Ideas and answers

## Chapter 1
### Activity 1.1
Some examples of regional differences you might notice include the following:

- A short vowel /ʊ/ in words such as 'roof' (eastern England) or in 'tooth' (Wales)

- A long vowel /iː/ at the end of words such as 'city' and 'tidy' (south Wales)

- A 'rounded' vowel (lips are rounded) in words such as 'work' (Wales)

- A more 'open' vowel (mouth starts in a more open position) in words such as 'load' or 'boat' (Birmingham/West Midlands)

- The vowel /uː/ in words such as 'book' and 'cook' (Liverpool, parts of Lancashire)

- No distinction between words such as 'Pam' and 'palm' (Edinburgh and other Scottish accents)

- A more 'open' vowel in the last part of words such as 'better' or 'Manchester' (Manchester). This is the lettER vowel mentioned in the activity.

- The NURSE vowel in New York speech can be pronounced as a diphthong (an example being 'thirty' sounding more like 'toidy').

- The monophthongisation of PRICE in Southern US English speech, so that 'time' sounds like 'tahm'.

- The monophthongisation of MOUTH in the Pittsburgh area of the US (example of 'downtown' sounding like 'dahntahn'). Barbara Johnstone and Scott Kiesling have written a lot on 'Pittsburghese'.

- The MOUTH vowel in Canadian English sounds close to (but not the same as) the GOAT vowel in some contexts, so 'couch' can sound a bit like 'coach'.

More examples can be found in Hughes, Trudgill and Watt (2012).

## Activity 1.3

Some of the accent-specific spellings in the poem include:

| From under't canal<br>Down't stairs<br>Over't top | Examples of Yorkshire definite article reduction, where 'the' gets reduced to 't' or 'th' |
| --- | --- |
| watter in watter-filled | Local pronunciation of 'water' |
| wi' a pigeon<br>wi' a lit-up hat<br>wi' heads | Omission of consonant sounds at the end of some words, so 'with' becomes 'wi' |

# Chapter 2

## Activity 2.1

The writers take a negative view of occupational jargon. In Text 2A, they are concerned about its aggressive and militaristic overtones, and in Text 2B about its ability to exclude and marginalise workers. Thorne also points out that much jargon is used to hide reality and to spread particular commercial ideologies into areas where they did not exist before.

In its defence, you might argue that jargon is a useful form of shorthand for people who are all on the same page (or, to avoid using jargon, who all share the same frame of reference) and can also speed up communication when everyone understands what is being referred to.

## Activity 2.4

Many of the headlines express shock and surprise about young people's language, suggesting that they are speaking an alien language. They tend to foreground the most obscure or concerning terms, and often claim that they are used more widely than they are. Sex and drugs appear to be the prime concerns.

# Practice question

You could include a range of different points in an answer to a question like this, including:

- Social groups engage in similar activities together and develop a shared language.
- Social groups mark out their identity with a shared language, so it is not just the shared activity but the shared sense of belonging that influences language.

- People can belong to different groups and move between different styles or registers.

- Other factors – age, gender, region and individual language style – can actually be more important.

- It's worth examining what is meant by 'language' here too and to consider all the different aspects of it: vocabulary, syntax, phonology, morphology, pragmatics and even orthography.

# Chapter 3

## Activity 3.2b

Examples of shifts away from 'standard' English include the following:

**Phone call video**

- Pronunciation of 'theatre'

- 'Wassup dog'

- 'Dey all good singers'

- 'Alright' pronounced as 'aight'

**Obama meet and greet video**

In this video it is more to do with context. The phrases aren't necessarily non-standard, but they do represent something different from what is perhaps expected in the situation. There are of course also big differences in body language.

- 'Wassup fam?'

- Pronunciation of 'come on'

- 'Feel that?'

- 'Bring it in'

## Practice question

As with the practice question in Chapter 2, there are many different angles to a question like this.

- Ethnicity can play a large part in people's sense of identity, and language is an important aspect of that.

- Ethnicity need not 'always' play a part in language use because language users have choices over how they wish to perform their identities.

- Context might be more important than ethnicity in some situations and other factors – age, gender, social class and region – may all be significant.

- As the chapter suggests, for many (white) people, ethnicity is only apparent when attention is drawn to its 'marking' and there is an assumption that white people do not 'do' ethnicity.

- Is ethnicity being confused with other forms of identity and practice?

- As with social groups, it's important to consider what is meant by 'language' here too and to consider all the different aspects of it: vocabulary, syntax, phonology, morphology, pragmatics and even orthography.

- What do linguists have to say about this? Make sure you look at studies, research and theories put forward about the topic.

# Chapter 4

## Activity 4.1

While the words are recognisably English, many of the expressions mean very little or sound like they should be idiomatic expressions. The cards are deliberately designed to be nonsensical, so they demonstrate a playfulness with English.

## Activity 4.2

Most linguists agree that all modern languages share common ancestry in one language, Proto-Indo-European, although there are different theories as to where this originates from. In the British Isles, Celtic languages established themselves in pre-Christian times. Latin came with the Romans in 43 CE but it is hard to know how much either of these had an impact on the language that later became English (Anglo-Saxon or Old English).

## Activity 4.3

- Pyjamas: Urdu and Persian origin

- Bungalow: from Hindi and referring to a type of housing from Bengal (now Bangladesh)

- Assassin: originally from Arabic and then Latin and French, meaning 'hashish eater'

- Thug: from Sanskrit and then Hindi, meaning 'thief'

- Mohawk: from the Iroquoian language of Native Americans, now referring to a hair cut

- Tattoo: from Tahiti, Tongo and Samoa

- Kosher: from Hebrew

## Activity 4.4

The range of differences between Standard English and the varieties of English used in Wales, Scotland and Ireland is vast and would take too much space to explain in detail here. Chapters 5–8 of *Language in the British Isles* edited by David Britain (see References at the end of this book) offer a detailed overview of each variety with examples of lexical, phonological and syntactical variations.

## Activity 4.5

| UK | USA |
|---|---|
| *Flat:* Old English word for 'dwelling' | *Apartment:* used in USA in late nineteenth century, but originally from Latin via French |
| *Pavement:* Middle English word derived from French | *Sidewalk:* used in English in early eighteenth century, but seen as alternative to UK 'pavement' in early twentieth century |
| *Tramp:* from the verb 'to tramp' (describing walking around) in the mid-seventeenth century | *Bum/hobo:* 'bum' is seen in US use from mid-nineteenth century and possibly from a German word for a person who 'bums around', idles or loafs |
| *Lift:* from 1850s English use | *Elevator:* originally from Latin but used in both UK and US from the late eighteenth century as a mechanical device for lifting |
| *Trousers:* probably from Irish/ Gaelic in sixteenth century | *Pants:* from the word 'pantaloons' and around since 1840. In UK usage they refer to underwear but in US usage they mean what the UK would call trousers |

## Activity 4.6

In Texts 4A and 4B, the writers appear fairly fluent in formal written English but there are occasional moments when features such as determiners (*the* wrong conclusion) are not used or where tense is harder to construct ('Before the strike we *pay* for medical care'). Some spellings – *effect* (instead of *affect*) and *emparassment* (rather than *embarrassment*) – are also wrong and, in the case of Text 4B, there are more examples of grammatical problems in constructing complete sentences ('You see we are living like the third world people here but now after the strike.') and in subject – verb agreement ('Our Government said that *there were* no coal.').

# Practice question

A question like this encourages you to weigh up different arguments and consider the relative merits of each one. Many commentators argue that the range of differences in English around the world is a threat to the cohesiveness of the language, while others argue that the diversity and range is a strength that should be celebrated.

There is also a view that the differences between different World Englishes will inevitably lead to the fragmentation of English into different, mutually incomprehensible languages, as happened to Latin before.

The question itself puts similarities ahead of differences, though, perhaps encouraging you to think of arguments that foreground the shared characteristics of many World Englishes. English as a *lingua franca* would seem a good place to look here, as well as the shared grammatical structures and vocabulary of different forms.

As with other questions, it is important to look at what linguists have to say about these debates and to consider the models they propose.

## Activity 4.8

There is one example of idiomatic or business English in the text – 'ballpark figure' – meaning an approximate figure (based on the American use of 'ballpark' to mean a large area for sports). Expressions like this are problematic in international interactions because they are often idiomatic and therefore not literally translatable. Interactions with non-native speakers of English (or even with younger speakers of a language who might not have the same lexicon of idiomatic expressions) might be clearer if they were more literal.

# International phonetic alphabet (IPA) chart

| Consonants | | Vowels | |
|---|---|---|---|
| p | pip | **Short vowels** | |
| b | bib | ɪ | pit |
| t | ten | e | pet |
| d | den | æ | pat |
| k | cat | ɒ | pot |
| g | get | ʌ | but |
| f | fish | ʊ | book |
| v | voice | ə | mother |
| θ | thigh | **Long vowels** | |
| ð | this | iː | bean |
| s | set | ɜː | burn |
| z | zoo | ɑː | barn |
| ʃ | ship | ɔː | born |
| ʒ | measure | uː | boon |
| h | hen | **Diphthongs** | |
| tʃ | church | aɪ | bite |
| dʒ | judge | eɪ | bait |
| m | man | ɔɪ | boy |
| n | now | əʊ | toe |
| ŋ | sing | aʊ | house |
| l | let | ʊə | cure |
| r | ride | ɪə | ear |
| w | wet | eə | air |
| j | yet | | |

# References

Becker, K. (2014) 'Linguistic repertoire and ethnic identity in New York City', *Language & Communication* 35: 43–54.

Benor, S. B. (2010) 'Ethnolinguistic repertoire: Shifting the analytic focus in language and ethnicity', *Journal of Sociolinguistics* 14(2): 159–83.

Bernstein, B. (1971) *Class, Codes and Control: Theoretical Studies Towards a Sociology of Language*. London: Routledge & Kegan Paul.

Bobo, L. (2001) 'Racial attitudes and relations at the close of the twentieth century'. In N.J. Smelser, W.J. William and F. Mitchell (eds) *America Becoming: Racial Trends and Their Consequences*. Washington DC: National Academy Press 1: 264–301.

Britain, D. (ed.) (2007) *Language in the British Isles*. Cambridge: Cambridge University Press.

Chambers, J.K. and Trudgill, P. (1998) *Dialectology* (Second edition). Cambridge: Cambridge University Press.

Cheshire, J. (1982) *Variation in an English Dialect: A Sociolinguistic Study*. Cambridge: Cambridge University Press.

Cheshire, J., Nortier, J. and Adger, D. (2015) 'Emerging Multiethnolects in Europe', *QMUL Occasional Papers in Linguistics*, No 33. London: QMUL.

Coleman, J. (2012) *The Life of Slang*. Oxford: Oxford University Press.

Coulthard, M. (2004) 'Author identification, idiolect and linguistic uniqueness', *Applied Linguistics* 25(4): 431–447.

Crystal, D. (2003) *English as a Global Language* (Second edition). Cambridge: Cambridge University Press.

Crystal, D. (2012). 'Academic English', a video for Cambridge University Press ELT. Cambridge: Cambridge University Press. Available at: www.youtube.com/watch?v=hGg-2MQVReQ

Dent, S. (2016) *Modern Tribes: The Secret Languages of Britain*. London: John Murray.

Drummond, R. (2012) 'Aspects of identity in a second language: ING variation in the speech of Polish migrants living in Manchester, UK', *Language Variation and Change* 24: 107–133.

Drummond, R. (2016) '(Mis) interpreting urban youth language: white kids sounding black?, *Journal of Youth Studies* 20(5): 640–660.

Eckert, P. and McConnell-Ginet, S. (1992) 'Communities of practice: Where language, gender, and power all live'. In K. Hall, M. Bucholtz and B. Moonwomon (eds), *Locating Power, Proceedings of the 1992 Berkeley Women and Language Conference*. Berkeley: Berkeley Women and Language Group, 89–99.

Engel, M. (2010) 'Say no to the get-go! Americanisms swamping English, so wake up and smell the coffee', *The Daily Mail*, 29 May. Available at: www.dailymail.co.uk/news/article-1282449/Americanisms-swamping-English-wake-smell-coffee.html

Eckert, P. (2008) 'Where do ethnolects stop?', *International Journal of Bilingualism* (12) 1&2: 25–42.

Foulkes, P. and Docherty. G. (2007) 'Phonological variation in England'. In D. Britain (ed.) *Language in the British Isles*. Cambridge: Cambridge University Press, pp. 52–74.

Fox, K. (2005) *Watching the English: The Hidden Rules of English Behaviour*. London: Hodder & Stoughton.

Fox, K. (2010) 'Interaction between social category and social practice: explaining was/were variation', *Language Variation and Change* 22: 347–371.

Galloway, N. and Rose, H. (2015) *Introducing Global Englishes*. London: Routledge.

Green, J. (2010) *Green's Dictionary of Slang*. London: Chambers.

Hazel, S. (2016) 'Why native English speakers fail to be understood in English – and lose out in global business', *The Conversation*, February 10. Available at: https://theconversation.com/why-native-english-speakers-fail-to-be-understood-in-english-and-lose-out-in-global-business-54436.

Hickey, R. (2007) 'Southern Irish English'. In D. Britain (ed.) *Language in the British Isles*. Cambridge: Cambridge University Press pp. 135-151.

Holmes, J. and Wilson, N. (2017) *An Introduction to Sociolinguistics*. (Fifth edition). Oxon: Routledge, p. 35.

Hughes, A., Trudgill, P. and Watt, D. (2012) *English Accents and Dialects* (Fifth edition). London: Routledge.

Jenkins, J. (2006) 'Current perspectives on teaching world Englishes and English as a lingua franca, *TESOL Quarterly* 40(1): 157–181.

Jenkins, J. (2015) *Global Englishes: A Resource Book for Students* (Third edition). London: Routledge, p. 94.

Johnston, P.A. Jr (2007) 'Scottish English and Scots'. In D. Britain (ed.) *Language in the British Isles*. Cambridge: Cambridge University Press.

Leith, D. (2007) 'English – colonial to postcolonial'. In D. Graddol, D. Leith, J. Swann, M. Rhys and J. Gillen (eds) *Changing English*. London: Routledge, pp. 117–152.

Lippi-Green, R. (1997) *English with an Accent*. New York: Routledge.

Llamas, C. (2000) 'Middlesbrough English: Convergent and divergent trends in a "part of Britain with no identity"'. In *Leeds Working Papers in Linguistics and Phonetics*.

Lllamas, C. (2006) 'Shifting identities and orientations in a border town in Sociolinguistics of Identity. In T. Omoniyi and G. White (eds) *Continuum*, pp. 92–112.

Llamas, C. (2007) 'A new methodology: data elicitation for regional and social language variation studies', *York Papers in Linguistics,* 138–163.

Llamas, C., Mullany, L. and Stockwell, P. (2006) *The Routledge Companion to Sociolinguistics*. London: Routledge.

Mahdawi, A. (2017) 'I'm a bit brown. But in America I'm white. Not for much longer', *The Guardian,* 21

March. Available at: www.theguardian.com/commentisfree/2017/mar/21/us-census-whiteness-race-colour-middle-east-north-africa-america

Masters, S. (2013) 'George Osborne's "man of the people" accent ridiculed' *The Independent*, 26 June. Available at: www.independent.co.uk/news/uk/politics/george-osbornes-man-of-the-people-accent-ridiculed-8675419.html

Mencken, H. L. (2017) *The American Language: A Preliminary Inquiry Into the Development of English in the United States* (Classic Reprint) – a modern reprint of the 1919 original.

Milroy, J. and Milroy, L. (1978) 'Belfast: change and variation in an urban vernacular'. In P. Trudgill, *Sociolinguistic Patterns in British English*. London: E. Arnold, pp. 19–36.

Milroy, J. and Milroy, L. (1985) 'Linguistic change, social network and speaker innovation', *Journal of Linguistics* 21: 339–384.

Moore, E. (2011) 'I were out with Lucy last week. She were in a right good mood.' 3 October. Available at: http://linguistics-research-digest.blogspot.co.uk/2011/10/i-were-out-with-lucy-last-week.html

O'Riagain, P. (2007) '"Irish" in language in the British Isles'. In D. Britain (ed.), *Language in the British Isles*. Cambridge: Cambridge University Press, pp. 218–236.

Penhallurick, R. (2007) 'English in Wales'. In D. Britain (ed.) *Language in the British Isles*. Cambridge: Cambridge University Press.

Petyt, K. M. (1985) *Dialect and Accent in Industrial West Yorkshire*. London: John Benjamins Publishing.

Porter, H. (1995) 'Back Off, Ease Up, Enjoy', *The Guardian* (6 April 1995).

Rubin, D. (1992) 'Nonlanguage factors affecting undergraduates' judgments of non-native English-speaking teaching assistants', *Research in Higher Education* 33(4): 511–31.

Saraceni, M. (2011) 'Reflections on the rhetorics on the (Re-)Location of English', *Changing English* 18: 3: 277–285.

Savage, M., Devine, F., Cunningham, N., Taylor, M., Li, Y., Hjellbrekke, J., Le Roux, B., Friedman, S. and Miles, A. (2013) 'A new model of social class? Findings from the BBC's Great British Class Survey experiment', *Sociology*, 47 (2): 219–250.

Seargeant, P. (2012) *Exploring World Englishes: Language in a Global Context*. London: Routledge.

Seidlhofer, B. (2004) 'Research perspectives on teaching English as a lingua franca', *Annual Review of Applied Linguistics* 24: 209–239.

Sharma D. (2011) 'Style repertoire and social change in British Asian English', *Journal of Sociolinguistics* 15(4): 464–492.

Sharma, D. and Rampton, B. (2015) 'Lectal focusing in interaction: a new methodology for the study of style variation', *Journal of English Linguistics* 43(1): 3–35.

Swales, J. (1990) *The Concept of Discourse Community, Genre Analysis: English in Academic and Research Settings*. Boston: Cambridge University Press.

Trudgill, P. (1968) 'Sex, covert prestige and linguistic change in the urban British English of Norwich', *Language in Society* 1: 179–195.

Trudgill, P. (2001) *Sociolinguistic Variation and Change*. Edinburgh: Edinburgh University Press.

Van Herk, G. (2012) *What is Sociolinguistics?* Malden: Wiley-Blackwell.

# Glossary

**accent:** variation in pronunciation, often associated with a particular geographical region

**accommodation:** how people adjust their speech behaviours to match others; this can be aspects of accent, grammar, vocabulary and even the style of speech delivery

**alveolar ridge:** the hard area behind the top front teeth

**code-switching:** when speakers who speak two or more different languages switch from one to the other, often in mid-conversation depending on who they are talking to or what they wish to accomplish. Can also be used to refer to switching between dialects in the same language

**community of practice:** a group of people engaged in a shared activity or practice, whose language is shaped by the activities they are mutually engaged in

**count noun:** a noun which refers to separate items that can be counted

**covert prestige:** The less obvious or hidden prestige associated with the use of certain non-standard varieties of a language within particular social groups. Van Herk (2012: 55) calls it 'the linguistic equivalent of *street credibility*'

**crossing:** the practice of using particular features of speech that 'belong' to a different ethnicity from that of the speaker

**deficit model:** a way of describing a form of language as lacking, or deficient in, some quality – linguists tend to avoid such judgements

**descriptivism:** an approach to language study that focuses on how language is actually used

**dialect:** variation in words and structures associated with a particular geographical region (also includes accent)

**dialect levelling:** the process by which language forms of different parts of the country converge and become more similar over time, with the loss of regional features and reduced diversity of language

**diaspora:** a dispersal or spreading out from a central point

**discourse community:** a group of people with shared interests and belief systems who are likely to use language in similar ways

**diphthong:** a vowel which starts as one sound then changes to another. For example, the /ɔɪ/ vowel sound in the word 'choice'

**divergence:** when an individual changes their language choices (usually temporarily) to become more dissimilar to another individual or group

**downwards convergence:** a speaker's emphasis on the non-standard aspects of their speech emphasising the covert prestige of non-standard forms

**ethnicity:** a shared social identity consisting of cultural practices, language, beliefs and history. You have some control over your ethnic affiliation

**ethnolect:** a variety of language that is associated with a particular ethnic group

**ethnolinguistic repertoire:** a set of linguistic resources that are available to be used by individual speakers in order to signal their ethnic identity

**eye dialect:** the deliberate use of misspellings to identify a speaker who is using a regional or non-standard form of English. So called because we see rather than hear the difference

**field-specific lexis:** vocabulary that is only related to a particular field of work or activity

**General American (GA):** The majority accent in the USA, lacking any distinctly regional characteristics. It is an imprecise term that is used in linguistics mainly for comparison purposes

**heritage language:** a language that is not the dominant language in the society in which somebody lives, yet it is one that is spoken at home

**idiolect:** variation in language use associated with an individual's personalised 'speech style'

**idiom:** an expression or phrase that is commonly used but whose meaning is not literal (e.g. 'to kick the bucket' means 'to die'). Such expressions often have ancient historical origins

**intersectionality:** the idea that social categorisations are all interconnected and overlapping. Someone's ethnicity cannot be separate from their gender, social class, sexuality, and so on

**jargon:** the vocabulary and manner of speech that define and reflect a particular profession which may be difficult for others to understand

**lexical set:** a group of words which have the same vowel sound in a given variety of English. For example, if a particular variety uses /æ/ in the word 'bath', then it will also use /æ/ in other words within the lexical set (e.g. 'path', 'graph', etc). Each set is represented by a keyword which is usually written in SMALL CAPS

*lingua franca*: a language used to communicate between people who speak different languages

**marked:** something that stands out and is noticed as different from the norm

**mode:** the physical channel of communication: either speech or writing

**monophthong:** a vowel which has a single sound throughout its duration. For example, the /iː/ vowel sound in the word 'sheep'

**mother tongue variety:** the language that a person learns first as a child

**multiethnolect:** a collection of linguistic resources combining features from a variety of languages within a multi-ethnic, multicultural context

**non-count noun:** a noun which refers to something that cannot be counted or separated

**overt prestige:** the obvious prestige associated with the use of the standard variety of a language within a particular society. Connected to notions of speaking 'properly'

**phoneme:** the smallest individual unit of sound in a language which conveys a meaning, for example in 'fell' and 'well', the /f/ and /w/ sounds are phonemes

**postvocalic /r/:** the /r/ sound that appears after a vowel and before a consonant ('farm') or at the end of a word ('far'). It is not pronounced in most English accents

**prescriptivism:** an approach to language study that focuses on rules and notions of correctness

**race:** perceived physical similarities and differences that groups and cultures consider socially significant. You generally cannot choose your race

**Received Pronunciation (RP):** an accent in English which does not indicate a person's geographical location and which is recognised as having a high social status; RP is found throughout the English-speaking world

**repertoire:** a range of language features available for speakers to choose from

**rhotic accent:** an accent which pronounces postvocalic /r/

**sociolect:** the language used by a particular social group, e.g. teenage school children, adults in a book club

**style-shifting:** when speakers adjust the way they speak depending on a combination of factors such as how much attention they are paying to what they are saying, who they are talking to, or how they want to be perceived in a particular context

**th-fronting:** the pronunciation of 'th' as /f/ or /v/. So 'think' becomes 'fink' and 'with' becomes 'wiv'

**unmarked:** the common, regular, normal version of something that can go unnoticed

**upwards convergence:** a speaker's emphasis on the standard aspects of their speech emphasising the prestige of standard forms

# Index

# Acknowledgements

*The authors and publishers acknowledge the following sources of copyright material and are grateful for the permissions granted. While every effort has been made, it has not always been possible to identify the sources of all the material used, or to trace all copyright holders. If any omissions are brought to our notice, we will be happy to include the appropriate acknowledgements on reprinting.*

Text 1A 'The Meaning of Life' from *Now It Can Be Told* by Ian McMillan, published and used with permission by Carcanet Press; Texts 1B *The Broons* and 1C *Oor Wullie* ® © DC Thomson & Co. Ltd. 2017, used by kind permission of DC Thomson & Co. Ltd.; Text 1D excerpt from 'Only the dead know Brooklyn' by Thomas Wolfe, published in The New Yorker, 1935; Text 2A excerpt from article 'Why workplace jargon is a big problem' by Maddie Crum in the Huffington Post, licensed via PARS International; Text 2B excerpt from article 'Translated: the baffling world of business jargon' by Tony Thorne in The Conversation (theconversation.com), used under Creative Commons license and with approval from The Conversation; Table 2A based on data from a 2014 survey by YouGov; Section 2.2.2 excerpt from article 'George Osborne's 'man of the people' accent ridiculed' by Sam Masters, The Independent, used by permission of ESI Media; Section 2.3 definition from the Oxford English Dictionary, used by permission from Oxford University Press; Text 2C Daily Mail headlines used by permission of Solo Syndication; Text 4A excerpt from 'Don't talk garbage!' by Christopher Stevens in the Daily Mail, used by permission of Solo Syndication; Section 4.5.1 excerpt from article 'Say no to the get-go!' by Matthew Engel in the Daily Mail, copyright Matthew Engel, used with permission of the author; Section 4.5.1 excerpt from article 'Back off, ease up, enjoy' by Henry Porter in the Guardian, copyright Guardian News & Media 2017; Section 4.5.2 excerpt from article 'Being a native English speaker is globally useless if you can't speak other versions of English' by Spencer Hazel on Quartz, originally published by The Conversation (theconversation.com) 'Why native English speakers fail to be understood in English – and lose out in global business', used under Creative Commons license and with approval from The Conversation; Figures 4.3 & 4.4 Ngrams created in Google Books Ngram Viewer http://books.google.com/ngrams

Development of this publication has made use of the Cambridge English Corpus (CEC). The CEC is a multi-billion word computer database of contemporary spoken and written English. It includes British English, American English and other varieties of English. It also includes the Cambridge Learner Corpus, developed in collaboration with Cambridge English Language Assessment. Cambridge University Press has built up the CEC to provide evidence about language use that helps to produce better language teaching materials.

*Thanks to the following for permission to reproduce images:*

Cover image: Fitzer/Getty Images; chapter openers 1-4 Jamie Grill/Getty Images, Hy Peskin/Getty Images, Nick Dolding/Getty Images, Westend61/ Getty Images; Figure 1.2 RichLegg/Getty Images; Figure 3.1 Janine Wiedel Photolibrary/Alamy Stock Photo; Figure 3.4 David M. Benett/Dave Benett/ Getty Images for The Dean Collection/Bacardi; Figure 3.5 Joseph Okpako/ WireImage/Getty Images; Figure 4.1 Dan Clayton

The publisher would like to thank the following members of The Cambridge Panel: English who assisted in reviewing this book: Anisa Ravat, Carolin Haubold, Angela Janovsky.